Best Mets

WITHDRAWN MAY 2012

Best Mets

Fifty Years of Highs and Lows from New York's Most Agonizingly Amazin' Team

MATTHEW SILVERMAN

TAYLOR TRADE PUBLISHING

LANHAM · NEW YORK · BOULDER · TORONTO · PLYMOUTH, UK

Published by Taylor Trade Publishing
An imprint of The Rowman & Littlefield Publishing Group, Inc.
4501 Forbes Boulevard, Suite 200, Lanham, Maryland 20706
www.rlpgtrade.com

Estover Road, Plymouth PL6 7PY, United Kingdom

Distributed by National Book Network

British Library Cataloguing in Publication Information Available

Library of Congress Cataloging-in-Publication Data

Silverman, Matthew, 1965-
  Best Mets : fifty years of highs and lows from New York's most agonizingly
amazin' team / Matthew Silverman.
    p. cm.
  Includes index.
  ISBN 978-1-58979-670-6 (pbk. : alk. paper)
  1. New York Mets (Baseball team)—History. I. Title.
GV875.N45S549 2012
796.357'64097471—dc23

                                2011033206

∞™ The paper used in this publication meets the minimum requirements of
American National Standard for Information Sciences—Permanence of
Paper for Printed Library Materials, ANSI/NISO Z39.48-1992.

Printed in the United States of America

For Dana A. Brand (1954–2011)

Bard of the Mets, who searched inside the concrete of a dingy, multipurpose municipal facility in Queens and found the souls of millions of people residing there.

> For almost fifty years, Mets fans have been invited to "step right up" or "come to the park" and "Meet the Mets." Well, we've met the Mets. And they are us.
>
> —D. A. B., *The Last Days of Shea*

Contents

Acknowledgments

FIFTY YEARS OF METS BASEBALL is now in the books. In that time, the team has worn just about every hat possible: fool, miracle worker, believer, laughingstock, comeback kid, underachiever, disgrace, overachiever, hero, slacker, hacker, champ, chump, and underdog. And fans have stuck with the Mets throughout this epic journey. Not every fan has remained true—New Yorkers can be fickle—but the stands are still mostly filled with the hard core, the ones who don't give in, who don't leave early, who read the acknowledgments in a book on their club. Thank you.

Thanks also go out to the former Mets who provided me with their top-five Mets of all-time to use as a comparison with my top fifty. Number one on the list, Tom Seaver, is the same for everybody who has ever followed the Mets, but the other four picks are far from automatic. Thanks to Bud Harrelson, Keith Hernandez, Jerry Koosman, Ed Kranepool, Bobby Ojeda, and John Stearns for their thoughtful responses that were divined on the spot. And thanks to *USA Today Sports Weekly* for coincidentally publishing their survey's top five while I was tracking down the answers from the ex-Mets. Also thanks to Mets groundskeeper extraordinaire Pete Flynn and Eddie Boison, aka Cowbell Man, for talking with me for the "Mets People" profiles in this book. And thanks to the Mets for granting me field access when requested, notably during spring training in 2011.

The nature of a book like this is to tell the story as thoroughly as possible from many different perspectives. Events are repeated in a few places, but with the Mets the grand moments are worth savoring, and the disappointments you can't forget anyway.

Now that the action on the field is covered, there is the matter of those who helped make this book a reality. Thanks to Rick Rinehart, Flannery Scott, Alden Perkins, and the people at Taylor Trade, part of the Rowman &

Littlefield Publishing Group. This book would not be possible without the work of my agent, Anne Marie O'Farrell of Marcil-O'Farrell Literary LLC.

Then there is the inspirational part of the equation. I've been fortunate to have now worked on eight books on the Mets. Not many teams enjoy the unique history and perspective of the Mets, and none has the kind of fan base that so eagerly awaits the publication of each book. I have always taken my responsibility of chronicling this team as a matter of the highest order. I truly appreciate the opportunities afforded me and the support given me in the New York Metropolitan area—and I don't simply mean the tristate region. Beyond geography, the Mets community is thriving in cyberspace. Beyond the usual haunts for general Mets knowledge at ultimatemets.com, mets.com, metsblog.com, baseball-reference.com, and ESPN New York, independent Mets sites prosper. Several such sites are featured in this book: Centerfield Maz, Faith and Fear in Flushing, Mets by the Numbers, Mets Police, Mets Report, On the Black, and Ted Quarters. I would be remiss not to mention the sites that feature my work, including the Mets section at The Baseball Page and my personal blog at metsilverman.com. Additional thanks go to Greg Prince and Greg Spira for their help. Special thanks for generous photography assistance go to Jacob Kanarek, Dwayne Labakas, Tim Wiles at the National Baseball Hall of Fame Library, and, as always, Dan Carubia.

A few years ago, I had the distinction of finishing a book on the Mets while they were playing in the postseason. No playoffs this time—this book was completed while I coached my daughter's softball team, the Silverbacks, in the Rondout Valley Little League. The girls reminded me how hard and how much fun the game can be to learn and play. Thanks go to Kendall Becraft, Chantelle Bigler, Lindsay Harder, Jessica Meyer, Bianca Novotny, Sophia Pellegrini, Stella Picuri, Jessi Schlosser, Jan Silverman, Sasha Stratton, Baylee Szekeres, and Nicole Zeboris. Also, thanks go to the parents plus able assistants Fabian Meyer, Deb Silverman, and Elaine Szekeres. And what better omen for putting out a Mets book could there be than to have my Mets-mad son, Tyler, randomly assigned to don the Mets uniform in the Major-Minor League. Amazin' coincidence.

Fifty Never Felt So Young

S O YOU THOUGHT being a Mets fan was going to be easy? If you've been around for a while, or even for the whole fifty years of Mets existence, welcome again. If you're relatively new to all this, have a seat, get comfortable. As a Mets fan you won't be comfortable for long.

The Mets were born out of longing. The Brooklyn Dodgers and New York Giants owned the rights to the heart of the National League fans from the late 1880s through most of the 1950s. They both moved to California and left behind not so much as a "Dear John" note.

Attorney William A. Shea was charged with bringing National League baseball back to New York. He took on a league that was apathetic to expansion and unmoved concerning the relocation of New York's National League soul. That New York wound up with an NL team is because of Shea's diligence and his threat to start the Continental League. The NL finally concluded that it was better to let in New York and Houston—and take their money—than to deal with a third major league. (The American League also expanded, in 1961.)

The National League flotsam and jetsam made available to the Mets and Colt .45s (later the Astros) did not assure mediocrity, much less prosperity. George Weiss, who had maintained the Yankees as a powerhouse, took over running the Mets and made the dubious decision of picking recognizable names of veterans near the end of their careers rather than going with players who were unheard of yet might have a future. New York's best move was hiring Casey Stengel. Having a name manager proved quite useful. Creating a team from scratch was a daunting task, but the Mets had one of the game's most entertaining characters on the payroll, pitching his new club everywhere he went. The seventy-two-year-old Stengel had known unprecedented success with the Yankees until his abrupt "retirement," along with Weiss, in the wake of the 1960 World Series defeat. Now his team found "new ways to lose 'em I never knew existed before."

The Mets lost 400 games in less than four years under Stengel, starting with a staggering 120 losses in 1962 at the Polo Grounds and ending with Casey's broken hip on the eve of the manager's seventy-fifth birthday party at Shea Stadium in 1965. Wes Westrum took over the club, and, in 1966, the Mets avoided tenth place and 100 losses for the first time. The Mets reversed field in 1967, even as they introduced the league to one of the game's greatest pitchers in an era filled with great pitchers. Tom Seaver (16–13, 2.76 ERA) was the first Met to be an All-Star, to be an award winner (1967 NL Rookie of the Year), to surpass eleven wins, or to have an ERA below 3.00 over 162 or more innings. The Mets finally had an ace on the mound. What they needed was a leader in the dugout.

Gil Hodges had been one of those over-the-hill former Brooklyn Dodgers populating the first-year Mets roster. He hit the first home run in Mets history, but injuries necessitated the 1962 trade for Marvelous Marv Throneberry, a lead glove next to Gil's Gold Glove. The Mets sent Hodges to Washington to manage the expansion Senators in 1963; now the Mets wanted him back. Johnny Murphy, who would soon take over as general manager for the departing Bing Devine, arranged to return Hodges to his home in Brooklyn. Unlike the Dodgers, Gil had never left.

Hodges cleared out those who were unbothered by losing or who were unwilling to work his way. The 1968 Mets still couldn't hit—though hitting was at a premium in the "Year of the Pitcher"—but New York's pitching improved with the emergence of rookie southpaw Jerry Koosman and wild, hard-throwing Texas right-hander Nolan Ryan. After their first seventy-win season in 1968, improvement was expected at Shea Stadium, but no one saw a "Miracle" on the horizon.

⚾ Look Who's Number One ⚾

The 1969 Chicago Cubs were twenty games over .500 after just fifty-two games. Seaver, meanwhile, refused to celebrate the Mets' reaching .500 on May 21. The Mets got thumped the next night, 15–3, starting a five-game skid—their longest losing streak of the year. Many assumed the Mets would never see .500 again. Instead, the Mets reeled off eleven straight wins. New York then won two series from Chicago in successive weeks in July, including a perfect-game bid by Seaver, which was broken up in the ninth inning. (In their first half century, this was just about as close as the pitching-rich Mets would get to a no-hitter.)

In the days that followed Neil Armstrong's moon landing on July 20, 1969, the Mets started falling back to earth. They dropped ten games back and fell to third place. Beginning on August 16, the same weekend that a music festival called Woodstock clogged the New York State Thruway, the Mets began a run of eleven wins in twelve games. Though the Cubs started to show wear, Leo Durocher's veteran-laden club still held a seemingly firm five-game lead on September 3. A week later, the Mets were in first place.

Twice in a three-week span, the Mets set club records with extended shutout streaks: thirty-six consecutive scoreless innings from September 10–13 and then forty-two straight goose eggs from September 23–October 1, including the division-clinching shutout by Gary Gentry, another in a long line of Mets rookies who made the NL ill. Now the Mets took their summer stock blockbuster into October.

It almost seemed like the starting staff was given a well-deserved week off in the first National League Championship Series (NLCS). The hitters carried the load in the three-game sweep as the Mets outscored the Braves, 27–15. The Mets dropped the World Series opener to the heavily favored Baltimore Orioles, as the experts nodded in agreement. A team that started the season as 100-to-1 long shots to win the World Series, now had the odds where they wanted them.

The Mets evened the Series in Baltimore. They followed with a Gentry/Ryan combined shutout (aided by Tommie Agee's two miraculous catches), Seaver's ten-inning Game-4 gem (with a diving stab by Ron Swoboda and a ricochet off J. C. Martin's wrist proving the difference), and then came Kooz. Koosman, who'd taken a no-hitter into the seventh inning of Game

2, benefited from timely hitting and good fortune. In his two starts against Baltimore, light-hitting Al Weis provided crucial late-inning hits, and slugger Donn Clendenon homered in each game—his second blast came minutes after a smudge of shoe polish, supposedly belonging to Cleon Jones, started New York's rally from a 3–0 hole in Game 5. After Swoboda's double in the eighth gave the Mets the lead, two O's E's on one play put the Mets ahead 5–3. Seconds after Davey Johnson's flyball landed in Cleon's glove, Jerry Koosman landed in Jerry Grote's arms. The Miracle was complete.

While everything seemed to happen so fast at the end of the 1960s, the 1970s seemed to be in slow motion or, at the very least, repetitive. The Mets churned out identical 83–79 third-place finishes in 1970 and 1971. It proved to be a lot harder to win when the Mets couldn't sneak up on anyone. One of the great tragedies in team history caught everyone off guard. Gil Hodges died of a heart attack after playing golf with his coaches on Easter Sunday, 1972.

The idea that this regime change might not be a seamless transition became apparent early, when the Mets called a press conference to announce the acquisition of Rusty Staub and the hiring of Yogi Berra to be held the same afternoon that Hodges was laid to rest. Wes Westrum had been chosen to be manager instead of Berra in 1965, Yogi's first year as a Mets coach. After Westrum floundered, Gil Hodges got the job over Yogi. Though everyone from pitching coach Rube Walker to farm director Whitey Herzog was mentioned as a possible replacement, Berra was the most likely hire. And the team responded, winning twenty-three of their first thirty games to take a 6½-game lead. Injuries caught up to the Mets as they sagged in the second half, finishing 13½ games out—a twenty-game flip in the standings after mid-May. When the injuries continued in 1973 and the losses piled up, it looked like Berra might not be in the Mets dugout for long. But a relief pitcher made everyone believe.

Tug McGraw began his Mets career as a starter during Casey Stengel's regime and was converted to a reliever by Gil Hodges. Tug was the culprit during the team's dismal first five months and the hero in the final month. The Mets finished 21–8 with McGraw serving as inspiration, chanting "Ya Gotta Believe" and slapping mitt on thigh like a man possessed—hey, 1973 was the year *The Exorcist* was made. The Mets flew past the other five teams in the NL East, put a "Ball on the Wall," and knocked off the Cubs again, with a division title and the season on the line—though this time the main competition came from Pittsburgh and St. Louis. Jerry Koosman, who tossed 31⅔ consecutive shutout innings as the Mets made their push, won the game at Wrigley Field that earned at least a tie for first. Seaver won the next day, with McGraw—fittingly—getting the final seven outs for the unlikeliest of division titles, with an 82–79 record.

Pushing past mediocre competition in the division was one thing, but it was hard to believe the Mets could knock off the Big Red Machine in a best-of-five series. The Reds had been to the World Series in 1970 and 1972, losing both times. This time they did not get past the NLCS. Seaver, Koosman, and Jon Matlack each won once, with Rusty Staub clubbing three home runs and Bud Harrelson getting clubbed by Pete Rose in Shea's most memorable title bout. The ballpark was torn to pieces moments after McGraw got the last out in Game 5. There was more riot than reverie this time.

The defending-world-champion A's took advantage of second baseman Felix Millan's error to win the opener; the A's returned the favor with two miscues by their second baseman, Mike Andrews, the next day in the twelfth inning. A's owner Charlie Finley tried to get Andrews to feign an injury to get him off the roster, a move refused by the commissioner and an act that proved the last straw for A's manager Dick Williams, who wound up quitting the day the World Series ended. The Mets left New York after Game 5 needing one win for their second world championship. Their next World Series win would not come for thirteen years.

☻ Down Time ☻

The 1973 pennant was far more of a fluke than the 1969 Miracle. The Mets did little to improve the team after the 1973 World Series loss, and New York played poorly for five months in 1974. This time the Mets' late run ran smack-dab into a Pirates team that shooed them off like a fly. The Mets finished fifth, their first losing season in six years.

The Big Three of Seaver-Matlack-Koosman rolled along in 1975. Tom Terrific struck out two hundred batters for a record eighth straight year and claimed his third Cy Young Award, becoming the first right-hander to do so. Even with Felix Millan becoming the first Met to play in every game and setting a club record with 191 hits, plus Dave Kingman clubbing home runs to set the new franchise mark with thirty-six (thirteen in July alone), the Mets could not save Yogi Berra's job. With Roy McMillan filling out the lineup card, Skip Lockwood emerged as the late-inning successor to the traded McGraw, and recent callup Mike Vail tied the Mets record by hitting in twenty-three straight games.

With minor league manager Joe Frazier promoted to New York in 1976, the team's promising outfield of a year earlier—Cleon Jones, Del Unser, and Rusty Staub—was gone not long after the July 4 bicentennial. Vail proved both brittle and mediocre. Kingman, whose thirty clouts by the All-Star break brought up talk of Roger Maris's 1961 pace, got hurt and wound up with thirty-seven homers. Bruce Boisclair, with a .287 average and a unique batting stance, turned out to be, well, Bruce Boisclair. Lee Mazzilli was more of the speed-power combination the Mets were seeking, and the center fielder homered in his second at bat in the majors in September. Later that month, Kooz joined the twenty-win club for the first time and wound up second in the Cy Young voting. But 1976 was where the good times ended in New York for Koosman, his teammates, and the fans.

With the coming of free agency, player contracts had become a larger topic in the newspapers and an increasing cause of angst in the front office. Rusty Staub's approaching status as a "10-and-5 man"—a decade in the majors and five years with one team—resulted in his being traded to Detroit in December 1975 for washed-up southpaw Mickey Lolich. With the death of owner Joan Payson earlier that year, Board Chairman M. Donald Grant ran the team penuriously—and ran it into the ground.

Grant did sign Seaver, and even that was a problem. Arguably the best pitcher in the game, Seaver grew uneasy with his three-year deal as other pitchers without his pedigree leapfrogged him. Grant was infuriated by Seaver's words and used Dick Young of the *Daily News* to spread venom to the public. Dave Kingman's request for a lucrative deal along the lines of Reggie Jackson's Yankees contract fell on deaf ears, while the criticism of Jon Matlack and other players for not upgrading the offense through free agency only set Grant further on edge. When the standoff ended, Grant was still standing and the players were gone—gone too were the fans.

The ninety-eight-loss 1977 season was the last in New York for fan favorites Seaver, Kingman, Matlack, John Milner, Jerry Grote, Felix Millan, and Bud Harrelson. Koosman would have to wait another year—going

8–20 and 3–15 in the process—until he was dispatched at his insistence. Ed Kranepool, the last original Met and holder of most team records, retired after the 1979 season. (Mercifully, the mascot Mettle the Mule was also put out to pasture.) Seaver and Kingman returned in the early 1980s, but by then the damage was far too ingrained for any reunion to fix.

Seven consecutive sub-.500 seasons sapped the life from the franchise. Even the record $21.1 million sale of the club in 1980 to Nelson Doubleday and Fred Wilpon, a minority owner who served as president, did little to improve the team's fortunes on the field. General Manager Frank Cashen, whose Orioles had fallen to the Mets in the 1969 World Series, started from scratch in New York. Cashen kept Joe Torre, who, in 1977, had become the only Met promoted from the field to the manager's chair. Torre had just one season in which the team competed after August—and that was because of the 1981 strike.

The otherwise cataclysmic strike gave new life to the Mets, who had been fifteen games out and seventeen games under .500 when the players walked out in June. The Mets hung in the race in the second half despite finishing four games under .500—or twenty-one games under overall, depending on how you kept track of that convoluted campaign. Cashen was unimpressed and fired Torre, whose clubs had finished last as many times as Casey Stengel's. Torre had surpassed Stengel for most defeats in Mets history.

Torre's replacement turned out to be worse, though George Bamberger did not stick around long enough to threaten Torre's mark of 420 losses (only Bobby Valentine would pass that mark, and he did so in 1,003 games). Bamberger, who turned Milwaukee around before quitting due to a heart condition, took the Mets job as a favor to old friend Cashen and often looked like he couldn't wait for his part of the bargain to end. But 1982 got off to a promising start, even as big-name acquisition George Foster fizzled after receiving baseball's biggest contract. New York was playing .500 ball as late as June 25—and then the bottom dropped out. The Mets threatened Stengel's twenty-year-old record by dropping fifteen straight games and finished with ninety-seven losses. Bambi contemplated quitting, but he came back for more in 1983.

Mets fans also came back, packing Shea Stadium for the return of Tom Seaver on Opening Day. Darryl Strawberry, the first pick in the 1980 draft, arrived in May and went on to slug twenty-six homers and claim NL Rookie of the Year. But wins were scarce. After dropping a fourteen-inning game at Dodger Stadium to stand at 16–30, Bambi ran away. Coach Frank Howard took over, and the Mets showed glimpses of being a solid club—and then they would promptly go into a tailspin. Mookie Wilson scored ninety runs and stole fifty bases for the second straight year for a last-place club. He stole two wins in four days when he scored from second base in New York's last at bats on balls that didn't leave the infield. The winner in both games was Jesse Orosco, finally blossoming as a closer after the Mets traded wearisome reliever Neil Allen. That trade created stability in the pen *and* on the infield in one fell swoop.

Keith Hernandez was a perennial Gold Glove winner, the previous year's World Series hero, a batting champ, and the 1979 NL co-MVP. His partying ways had put him on the outs in St. Louis. Cardinals General Manager Joe McDonald, who as Mets GM had traded Seaver in 1977, shipped Hernandez to New York for Allen and pitching prospect Rick Ownbey on June 15, 1983. The trade jump-started the long-awaited resurgence of Mets baseball. It gave the Mets a true number-three hitter, while mercifully ending the necessity for defense from Dave Kingman, who had become the first Met to win a home-run crown in 1982—while batting just .204 with eighteen errors.

The burgeoning farm system would earn the Mets the *Baseball America* Organization of the Year in both 1983 and 1984. Along with several in-their-prime veterans who had survived the lean years, the Mets actually seemed on the way up. All they needed was a good manager and an ace to replace Seaver, who was gone again—this time due to a free-agent compensation snafu.

⚾ Goodenough ⚾

Though Frank Cashen had misfired in his first pick to manage the club, he would not squander his second chance. Davey Johnson, second baseman for Cashen's powerhouse Orioles teams of the late 1960s and early 1970s, had been coaxed out of the real estate business to be an instructor and manager in the Mets farm system. While managing at Triple-A Tidewater in 1983, Johnson saw a raw-boned eighteen-year-old come to the Tides from Class A. The kid could throw a ball through a wall, spin a knee-buckling curve, and showed the poise of a veteran. Not long after he was named to manage the Mets, Johnson started working on Cashen to put Dwight Gooden on the Opening Day roster.

Cashen was reluctant. He had let Joe Torre talk him into bringing the organization's top prospect, Tim Leary, to the big club in 1981. On a frigid afternoon during that season's opening series at Wrigley Field, Leary's elbow stiffened. He did not make his first start at Shea until 1983. Gooden now joined Leary in the 1984 starting rotation, but Leary lost his rotation spot in May—by then Gooden was well on his way to becoming the most-feared pitcher in the National League.

The idea of teams being afraid to face the Mets seemed ludicrous. Before agreeing to remain with the Mets, Hernandez had considered Shea Stadium to be "Baseball Siberia," but Mex and his mates soon learned that the team had passionate fans—1,829,482, to be exact, the most to come to Shea since the 1973 pennant season. Mets fans started the East Coast version of "The Wave," created Gooden's "K Korner," and littered the field with footwear on Flip Flop Night as a tribute to Hubie Brooks at the end of his club-record twenty-four-game hitting streak. A rookie bumper crop of Gooden, Ron Darling, Sid Fernandez, and Mike Fitzgerald, plus a host of under–twenty-five Mets, hijacked first place for sixty-five days and took it for a joy ride, stopping all over the country, including San Francisco, where four Mets were named All-Stars and Gooden struck out the side. The Cubs took back first place in August and claimed their first postseason berth since 1945, but no one was laughing at the Mets any more.

After winning ninety games, the second-highest total in Mets history next to the 1969 squad, the Mets looked for the next step. They sent regulars Brooks and Fitzgerald, plus two top prospects, to Montreal for Gary Carter, the premier catcher in the National League. Carter homered to win his first game as a Met on Opening Day and became the first Met to hit thirty home runs and drive in one hundred in the same year. Howard Johnson, acquired from Detroit in the off-season, proved to be an offensive machine—in odd-numbered years.

The freakish 1985 season included a 26–7 loss, a 16–13 win (in nineteen innings), a dozen 1–0 games (the Mets went 6–6), the Pittsburgh drug trials (with Keith Hernandez called to testify), and a two-day baseball strike, but the oddest thing about 1985 is that there were actually games that Dwight Gooden started and the team lost. Gooden won the pitching Triple Crown with a 1.53 ERA, 268 strikeouts, and a 24–4 record (18–1 after Memorial Day). At age twenty, he became the youngest twenty-game winner ever and was the unanimous pick for the Cy Young Award. For all the team's ninety-eight wins, however, the Mets needed one more victory in St. Louis in the last week of the season. The Mets took the first two games—including an eleven-inning 1–0 win on Darryl Strawberry's home run off the scoreboard clock—but the Cardinals held on for a one-run victory in the series finale. The Mets fell short, but the youngest and hardest-throwing pitching staff in the major leagues—their average age was under twenty-five—was battled tested. Look out, 1986.

The Mets began the season with a 2–3 mark, and suddenly they disappeared like a cartoon puff of smoke, leaving the rest of the National League behind. The Mets increased their win total for the sixth straight year—New York was ten wins better than the previous year and up fifty-three wins from 1982. The top-four pitchers in winning percentage were members of New York's starting rotation, led by 18–5 Bobby Ojeda, acquired from the Red Sox over the winter. The Mets still had the youngest staff in the majors (25.5), plus the lowest ERA (3.11) and most strikeouts (1,083). Everything they did seemed to work. When Davey Johnson wanted more pop, he inserted his power lineup with Howard Johnson—or even barrel-chested rookie Kevin Mitchell—at shortstop. Late in the year, the Mets brought up slick-fielding, twenty-one-year-old Kevin Elster to play shortstop after Rafael Santana was batted for in games by the likes of HoJo, Mitch, or Maz (the Mets got back Lee Mazzilli and released George Foster).

The Mets even won most of the fights they started. A memorable brawl occurred in Cincinnati—on a road trip that began with four Mets arrested for brawling at a Houston bar. After a dropped flyball enabled the Mets to tie the game in the ninth, Eric Davis slid into Mets third baseman Ray Knight in the tenth. The resulting fight—plus an earlier ejection of Darryl Strawberry—forced the Mets to put Gary Carter at third base, Ed Hearn behind the plate, Jesse Orosco in right field, and Roger McDowell on the mound. When a lefty came up, however, Orosco came in and McDowell went to the outfield, alternating in left or right field with Mookie Wilson. The Mets won when shortstop HoJo clubbed a three-run homer in the fourteenth.

The Mets scored more (783), walked more (631), and hit more (.263) than any National League club. They also wrapped up their division quicker than any team (September 17), and their fans had the clumps of the rampaged field to prove it.

It was a whole different world come October. Former Met Mike Scott beat Gooden in the opener, 1–0. But the Mets won three times in their last at bat: on Lenny Dykstra's two-run homer in the ninth in Game 3, on Gary Carter's RBI single in the twelfth in Game 5, and the piece de resistance, an RBI single in the top of the fourteenth in Game 6. But wait, Billy Hatcher's home run off the foul pole tied the game in the bottom of the inning. The Mets pushed three runs across in the sixteenth, and Orosco, running on fumes, allowed two runs in the bottom of the sixteenth. When Kevin Bass swung over Messy Jesse's 3–2 curve with the tying and winning runs aboard, the Mets had won the pennant. Orosco got the win in each of the three come-from-behind Mets victories. The specter of Scott, the Championship Series MVP, pitching a potential Game 7, pushed the Mets at the Astrodome just as the memory of the bitter ending to 1985 had pushed the Mets to dominate the National League all year.

The Mets got off to another slow start against Boston in the World Series. After dropping the first two games at Shea, they evened matters at Fenway behind Ojeda and Dykstra in Game 3 and Darling and Carter in Game 4. Bruce Hurst beat the Mets for the second time in Game 5, but the tenacious Ojeda went toe-to-toe with ex-teammate and AL MVP Roger Clemens in Game 6. Neither parachutists, nor premature MVP announcements, nor even being one out from losing could stop the Mets in the tenth inning. In Game 7, the sixth was the magic inning, with Hernandez getting the Mets back in the game against Hurst, whose name had been flashed on the scoreboard as World Series MVP ever so briefly in the previous game. Ray Knight, who hit a tiebreaking home run in Game 7, wound up getting the MVP trophy, and the Mets got a champagne bath.

⌒ Encore Falls Flat ⌒

Dwight Gooden missed almost two months after testing positive for cocaine, and the pitching staff was as fragile in 1987 as it had been hearty in '86. The Mets would not have reached ninety wins for the fourth straight year without an 11–1 season from swingman Terry Leach, who set a club record by winning his first ten decisions of the year. The three million who paid their way through Shea's gates—the first New York team to reach that attendance milestone—were treated to an offensive show like no one had seen before. Mets fans weren't alone. "The Year of the Home Run" saw 301 more home runs hit in the National League than were hit the previous year. Howard Johnson, the everyday third baseman after Knight was not retained as a free agent, hit twenty-six more home runs and knocked in sixty more runs than he did in 1986—giving him totals of thirty-six and ninety-nine in those categories, plus thirty-two steals. Strawberry's thirty-nine homers and thirty-six steals made the 1987 Mets the first team ever with 30-30 teammates. Kevin McReynolds, acquired in the blockbuster deal that sent Kevin Mitchell west, hit twenty-nine home runs and Carter blasted twenty. The team's 192 homers shattered the record of 148 set the previous year; the .268 batting average also was a new mark.

Yet it was the Cardinals, the only team in baseball without at least one hundred home runs in 1987, who received a dramatic homer from Terry Pendleton at Shea in September with the Mets poised to climb within a half game of first place. New York never got there. St. Louis scratched out its third division title—and pennant—in six seasons.

As they'd done in 1986, the Mets cleared the decks in 1988. The Mets wound up running away with the division title, but they poured it on late. The Mets never relinquished the lead after the first week of May, turning a four-game lead in mid-August into fifteen games by year's end. The one-hundred-win Mets led the NL in home runs (152), RBI (659), runs (703), on-base percentage (.325), and slugging (.396), plus the pitching was back in top form.

The club's major league–best 2.91 ERA was second in Mets history to 1968's 2.72 mark in the "Year of the Pitcher"—and given that 1987 had been the "Year of the Home Run," this Mets staff trumped the accomplishment of twenty years prior. But the home run came back to bite the 1988 Mets.

The Mets knocked out Orel Hershiser in the ninth inning of the opening game of the NLCS, the first time he'd been scored off since starting his record streak of fifty-seven consecutive scoreless innings. Carter's double off Jay Howell brought in the tying and go-ahead runs. That would not be the most memorable ninth-inning rally of the series.

The Mets held a two games to one lead at Shea and led 4–2 in the ninth in Game 4. The Mets had set a record with fifty-six home wins and had beaten the Dodgers ten of eleven times during the regular season, but this was not the regular season. Mike Scioscia's homer off Dwight Gooden tied the game, and Kirk Gibson's blast off Roger McDowell decided the game in the twelfth. David Cone, 20–3 during the year, tossed a five-hitter to force a seventh game, but Hershiser threw his own five-hitter the next night to send the Mets packing.

Over the next year, the Mets shipped out the nucleus that had helped win a championship. Wally Backman was traded in December 1988. The 1989 season would be the last in New York for Dykstra, McDowell, Hernandez, Carter, Mookie Wilson, Lee Mazzilli, and Rick Aguilera. Management wanted fewer partiers and more grind-it-out players like Gregg Jefferies, who'd come up in late August of 1988 and forced his way into the infield with his bat. Management didn't take into account the locker room dynamic—or defense. The end result was that the Mets didn't win.

The Mets finished second for the fourth time under Johnson in 1989. When the club got off to a 20–22 start in 1990, Davey Johnson, the winningest manager in Mets history, was fired. Bud Harrelson, veteran of the 1969 and 1973 Mets and a longtime coach, took over and the team took off. They gamely fought off injuries to stay with the Pirates most of the year, but even twenty wins from Frank Viola, nineteen by Dwight Gooden, a breakout .328 season by Dave Magadan, and Darryl Strawberry's thirty-seven homers and career-best 108 RBI weren't enough. Viola and Gooden were never that good again and Strawberry . . . well, Strawberry left.

In a move both sides would regret, Strawberry returned to his native Los Angeles and fell off the path that had once seemed destined for the Hall of Fame. Replacement Vince Coleman flopped as did a Hubie Brooks encore. Howard Johnson was superb in 1991, leading the league with thirty-eight homers and 117 RBI, and picking up his third 30-30 season in the process. The Mets still had a solid starting rotation with Gooden, Viola, and Cone—Fernandez was hurt, Darling was removed from the picture in a June trade, and Ojeda had been dealt in the off-season—but the Pirates were simply better than the Mets. Everyone else was passing them as well. The Mets went just 5–23 in one excruciating summer stretch, including a perfectly imperfect 0–10 road trip. Even Cone's nineteen-strikeout season finale in Philly could not rescue the Mets from fifth place, their worst finish and first losing season in eight years.

With Frank Cashen stepping down as general manager, and longtime assistant Joe McIlvaine in San Diego, the Mets tabbed Al Harazin to be the club's first new GM in a dozen years. Jeff Torborg, on the other hand, became the fourth new manager in the last two seasons. Harazin made splashy moves, bringing in Bret Saberhagen and shipping out McReynolds and Jefferies (his days were numbered after faxing his gripes to WFAN). The checkbook got a workout, bringing in veterans Willie Randolph and Eddie Murray, plus a $27.5 million contract for five years of Bobby Bonilla. Not only did the moves not pan out, but the Mets then traded their best pitcher over the last five seasons, David Cone, to Toronto in August 1992. Another frustrating fifth-place season became the basis for the book, *The Worst Team Money Could Buy*. But that name proved premature and fifth place seemed a pipe dream in 1993.

Torborg was gone by Memorial Day, and Harazin resigned a month later with the team twenty-six games under .500 and 26½ games behind. In the only seven-team alignment in NL history, the Mets finished seventh in the East, five games behind the expansion Marlins (and that was after a season-ending sweep of Florida). The 103 losses were the most in base-ball and the most by the franchise since 1965. Anthony Young set a major league record with twenty-seven consecutive losses over two seasons. But that was easier to take than the asinine behavior of Vince Coleman, laughing as he threw a firecracker that injured a toddler, and Bret Saberhagen, spraying bleach on reporters. McIlvaine, back in New York and finally the GM at Shea, had his work cut out for him.

Manager Dallas Green took the Mets through the strike that swallowed the end of the 1994 season and the first eighteen games of 1995. Yet, the Mets started to sort out some things. Bobby Jones was a reliable starter, Todd Hundley could hit, Rico Brogna was fun to watch and had a name that was fun to say, Edgardo Alfonzo could play second base superbly, and Jeff Kent could not play third base at all. Acquired from the Blue Jays in the 1992 Cone trade, Kent's only full season in New York was the club's horrific 1993 season, when he hit twenty-one home runs, knocked in eighty, and batted .270. Each of the other four years he spent in New York were truncated, including his 1996 season, when the Mets moved him unsuccessfully to third base and then moved him—even more unsuccessfully—to Cleveland with Jose Vizcaino for Carlos Baerga.

Green's denigrating of "Generation K"—a trio of heralded young pitchers who showed flashes of brilliance but proved ineffective and injury prone in New York—wound up costing the manager his job. Even with offensive club records falling all over the place—Hundley launched forty-one home runs, Lance Johnson amassed 227 hits and twenty-one triples, and Bernard Gilkey rapped forty-four doubles and tied a five-year-old Mets mark with 117 RBI—the club's pitching looked as sickly as some players did from room service during the first regular-season series in Mexico.

While McIlvaine bore responsibility for the failures of the Mets to capitalize on a successful second half of 1995, two Joe Mac decisions helped transform the Mets. He took a chance on John Olerud, whom Toronto was so eager to get rid of that they threw the Mets $5 million to take him. And McIlvaine brought Bobby Valentine back to New York.

⚾ Bobby V. for Victory ⚾

Bobby Valentine and pitching coach Bob Apodaca, who'd played for the 1970s Mets, put together a no-name staff that produced no results during the first two weeks of the 1997 season. The Dodgers came to Shea to celebrate the fiftieth anniversary of Jackie Robinson's breaking the color barrier on April 15, 1947. With President Bill Clinton and Jackie's widow, Rachel, on the field for a mid-game ceremony, Commissioner Bud Selig announced that Robinson's number, 42, would be retired in "perpetuity."

Whatever the effect on the team from that night, the Mets played like a different team. New York had the second-best record from that point forward (85–65), including three wins in their first four games at Atlanta's new Turner Field and shutting out the Yankees in the first-ever interleague meeting between the clubs (long-term success against either Atlanta or the Yankees would prove elusive).

Olerud was a rock in the middle of the order (102 RBI) and Alfonzo, shifted to third base, thrived batting in front of him. Rick Reed, a former replacement player, Rockies refugee Armando Reynoso, and All-Star Bobby Jones were low key and effective. John Franco led an effective bullpen. Even shortstop Rey Ordonez, who continued to prove that he couldn't hit, was simply spectacular in the field. And mercurial Carl Everett was a solid out-fielder, if not a solid citizen.

The eighty-eight wins in 1997 were a revelation, but in a city where the Yankees had resumed their championship swagger, being an underachiever wasn't a big selling point. A beam collapse at Yankee Stadium in April 1998 led to a hastily arranged Yankees-Angels afternoon game at Shea, while the Mets hosted their regularly scheduled night contest against the Cubs. Both home teams won, but the Yankees outdrew the Mets at Shea by almost twenty-five thousand. Despite catcher Todd Hundley being out of the lineup for the first half of the year, the Mets were initially reluctant to go after the best catcher in the game. But, by the start of Memorial Day week-end, Mike Piazza was a Met. The superstar era at Shea had begun.

The thumper helped the Mets stay in the race for the Wild Card until the final day, beginning a trend of last-day losses that would haunt the Mets over the next decade. The end of the 1999 season, however, would be worth remembering.

It didn't start out that way. General Manager Steve Phillips fired three of Valentine's coaches during a June series at Yankee Stadium. Al Leiter stopped both the club's eight-game losing streak and Roger Clemens's twenty-game winning streak. The Mets put it together from that point on. Olerud, who'd set a Mets record by hitting .354 the previous year, set an-other mark with 125 walks. Edgardo Alfonzo set a new standard with 123 runs scored. Knocking them in was Mike Piazza, the first Met to surpass 120 RBI in a season—the second was third baseman Robin Ventura, who made "Mojo Risin" the theme for the team.

After dropping eight of nine games in the final two weeks, the Mets swept the last series of the season to force a one-game playoff in Cincin-nati. Again, Leiter came through, and so did Alfonzo, cracking a two-run home run in the first inning in Cincy and then clubbing a grand slam in a tie game in the ninth the next night in Arizona in the National League Division Series (NLDS). The home run that would echo from that series was hit by backup catcher Todd Pratt, clinching the first postseason series victory by the Mets since the 1986 World Series. The memorable moment from the NLCS against the Braves was a ball that left the yard, with the bat-ter not getting past first base without getting a hug in the rain. The homer negated, the game still won, "The Grand Slam Single" was embraced. The clock struck midnight in Atlanta as the Braves, who blew a five-run lead, came back to twice tie Game 6. The Braves won when Kenny Rogers walked Andruw Jones with the bases loaded.

New acquisition Mike Hampton didn't have a lot of luck—and in some cases, control—but he had his moments in his lone season in New York . . . Japan was a different matter. The Mets and Cubs opened the 2000 season in Tokyo, the first teams to play regular-season games in Japan. Benny Agbayani launched a tenth-inning grand slam to split the two-game set and cancel a waiting ticket to the minor leagues.

All season the Mets turned seemingly difficult moments to their advantage: When Rickey Henderson, a .315 hitter the previous season, went into a home run trot for what turned out to be a single, the Mets released him the next day, and Agbayani became a regular. When "Old Reliable" Bobby Jones couldn't get people out, he went to the minors and returned a new man, going 8–2 with a 3.98 ERA in the second half. When Rey Ordonez broke his arm and was out for the season, Melvin Mora took over at short, creating a formidable lineup, if a little-less-airtight defense. Steve Phillips spent the summer trying to find a better defensive shortstop, getting turned down by Cincinnati's Barry Larkin before trading Mora to the Orioles for Mike Bordick—a weak hitter despite homering his first time up as a Met.

The Mets made the postseason for the second season in a row, the first such repeat in club history. As the Wild Card team, they drew the ninety-seven-win Giants and lost both their starting right fielder, Derek Bell, and the NLDS opener. No matter. Timo Perez, who'd spent his professional career in Japan before 2000, stepped in as the leadoff hitter and batted .294 the rest of the series. New York's upset of San Francisco rested on the shoulders of unheralded heroes: Rookie Jay Payton, who singled in the winning run in the tenth inning of Game 2; Agbayani, who homered in the thirteenth to win Game 3; and Jones, who tossed a one-hit shutout the next afternoon in the clincher.

Fortune continued to smile on the Mets in the NLCS. Hampton tossed a gem in the first game, and the next night looked like it might get away from the Mets, but Payton knocked in the go-ahead run in the ninth. After the Cards won Game 3, the Mets set a postseason record with five doubles in the first inning of Game 4. The next night, Todd Zeile cleared the bases with a double in the fourth inning and NLCS MVP Hampton clicked down the outs to the first Mets' pennant since 1986.

All the little things that had worked in the Mets' favor went against them in the first all–New York World Series since 1956. Timo slowed up on a ball that hit the wall and was thrown out at the plate, base runners missed chances to score tack-on runs, and Armando Benitez walked the leadoff batter with a one-run lead. The Yankees wound up winning in the twelfth. The next night, Roger Clemens threw a shattered bat at Mike Piazza, a reprise of their beanball episode in the Bronx in July. The Mets fell in a deep-enough hole that a five-spot in the ninth still left them a run short. The Mets ended the Yankees' World Series fourteen-game winning streak, but the Yankees won the next night and stood poised for the unthinkable: celebrating a world championship at Shea. Al Leiter, with three postseason wins in two years blown for him by Benitez, pitched until the game was decided. Luis Sojo hit a slow-hop single to snap a ninth-inning tie. The unthinkable was unleashed.

A season that seemed lost turned around in September 2001 for the Mets. And then everything was shattered. The September 11 tragedy took the lives of three thousand people and essentially shut down the country for close to a week. Just like people at other jobs, ballplayers struggled to return to normal. Ten days after the attacks, Shea Stadium, the site of relief efforts in the area after the attack, was ready for baseball again. The first post–9-11 outdoor sporting event in New York was an emotional evening with a climactic finish. Mike Piazza's two-run home run in the eighth inning gave the Mets a 3–2 win and provided a little something extra for people still dealing with many different emotions. The Mets, who'd donated a day's pay for widows and orphans and volunteered to help pack supplies—coordinated by Valentine—eventually fell short on the field in 2001, but they came through where it counted.

⚾ Down, Down, Down, and Up Again ⚾

If pennants were won by good press during the winter, the 2002 Mets would have claimed a pennant. Steve Phillips disposed of the trusted players who'd produced for the Mets in favor of good players gone bad: Mo Vaughn, Roberto Alomar, Jeromy Burnitz, Roger Cedeno, among others.

The 2002 team tanked, lost in a haze of bad trades, bad play, and marijuana smoke trailing off a few players. The Mets went an entire month without winning at home, tumbling from contender to disaster. The Mets lost fifteen straight at home in August, though they played .500 ball the final month and ended the year with a 6–1 win over the Braves. It turned out to be the last win by Bobby Valentine in a Mets uniform.

It did not, however, turn out to be the final game of the Steve Phillips regime. Ownership, now a purely Wilpon family entity after the buying out of Nelson Doubleday, chose to keep Phillips and oust Valentine. It also allowed Phillips to hire a manager, which was complicated by Seattle's not letting first choice Lou Piniella, still under contract to the Mariners, come to New York. Sweet Lou went to Tampa Bay—the Mets wound up with "Battlin' Art."

Howe had won three straight division titles with Oakland, as well as an American League record twenty straight games with the 2002 A's, yet GM Billy Beane asked for no compensation. Fred Wilpon liked the way Howe "lit up a room" and the manager liked his team for the way they "battled," as he repeated nightly in postgame interviews. The 2003 Mets lost the battle—and the war.

Jim Duquette replaced Phillips in June 2003 and immediately started trading many of the players that Phillips had brought to Shea. After the 66–95 campaign, the most defeats in a decade, some of the club's bally-hooed prospects were finally approaching the major league level.

Jose Reyes hit .307 in sixty-nine games with the Mets before an ankle injury ended his season. The twenty-year-old shortstop was clearly the best thing the team had going for it—Piazza missed most of the year with a groin injury—but the Mets inexplicably decided to move Reyes to second base in favor of Kaz Matsui, who came to America with a reputation of a strong arm and constitution, both of which he apparently left in Japan. By the end of 2004, David Wright was the third baseman, Reyes was back at short, Matsui was at second base . . . and the Mets were looking for a manager and GM. Again.

In July 2004, in the wake of the club's first sweep of the Yankees, the Mets opted to jump-start their plan and trade prospects for established ballplayers. The Mets brought in Kris Benson from the Pirates in exchange for Ty Wigginton and Jose Bautista, among others. The backbreaker, though, was trading their number-one draft pick of two years earlier, hard-throwing Scott Kazmir, for Tampa Bay's Victor Zambrano. Trading the prized lefty, often considered a future ace in Flushing, was one thing. Not getting back a legitimate number-one or -two starter, was another matter. The public was outraged, and the front office didn't wait for much more bad publicity or results. An eleven-game slide and losing nineteen of twenty-two sent both Howe and Duquette packing. The Mets needed a new plan, a new direction. And so they looked up an old friend.

Omar Minaya had left his assistant-GM post with the Mets two years earlier to take over the Montreal Expos, a ward of Major League Baseball. The Mets brought Omar back as a long-lost son and rewarded him with the checkbook. The Mets had tried to spend their way out of the basement in 1982 and again in 1992—it hadn't worked in either case. Now, with coveted All-Stars Carlos Beltran and Pedro Martinez fused with up-and-coming Wright and Reyes, plus Mike Piazza switching from first base back behind the plate, the Mets had a fresh look. They were, in the words of Beltran, "The New Mets."

Dropping five straight right off the bat was a stressful way for Willie Randolph to start his managerial career, but the Mets followed with six consecutive wins. These new Mets would be streaky all year. Cliff Floyd stayed healthy all season for the only time in his Mets career, but Mike Cameron was not so lucky. A frightening collision with Beltran in San Diego cost Beltran one series, though his performance suffered. Cameron was unable to reappear until the next year . . . ironically, as a Padre.

Pedro lived up to the billing early in his four-year deal, winning fifteen games—the bullpen blew five leads for him—and striking out 4.43 batters for every walk, the best mark in the National League. He won his two-hundredth career game early in 2006, but injuries to numerous body parts limited him for the rest of the year—and the rest of his contract. The 2006 Mets, however, made up for an old and banged-up rotation with a power-house pen: Billy Wagner, Duaner Sanchez, Chad Bradford, Darren Oliver, and holdover Pedro Feliciano. Tom Glavine, the elder statesman of the rotation—depending on whether you actually believe Orlando Hernandez's "official" age—won fifteen times and led the team with 198 innings. Rookie John Maine was the only regular Mets starter under the age of thirty-four. But whoever pitched, often had runs to work with.

Wright, Beltran, and Carlos Delgado became the first trio of teammates to homer twenty times before the All-Star Game; they would finish with 107 as a group. Reyes clubbed nineteen homers—and seventeen triples, plus he stole sixty-four bases—while reclamation project Jose Valentin hit eighteen home runs, including two in the division clincher at Shea on September 18. Yet, like the Mets of twenty years earlier, the 2006 Mets essentially wrapped up the title early, following a 9–1 road trip that pushed them 9½ games ahead before Father's Day. Atlanta bid farewell to its fourteen-straight division titles when the Mets swept the Braves at Turner Field at the end of July. It was the night of that last Braves game, after the Mets had flown to Miami, that things started to unravel. Duaner Sanchez broke his shoulder riding in a taxi and was out for the year. The Mets felt compelled to trade reliable right fielder Xavier Nady to Pittsburgh for reliever Roberto Hernandez and an erratic lefty named Oliver Perez.

The bullpen—and plenty of offense—carried the Mets in a Division Series sweep of the Dodgers. But the perennial Central champion Cardinals had better pitching and better luck. The series turned on a triple by Scott Spiezio that tied Game 2. So Taguchi won it in the ninth with a home run off Billy Wagner. The Cardinals took the series lead in St. Louis, but Maine beat the Cards in Game 6 to force a deciding game. With no one else to turn to, Randolph started Perez, who'd won just once as a Met before Game 4. It was tied when Scott Rolen's sixth-inning blast looked destined for the bullpen. Endy Chavez, playing in place of the hobbled Floyd, went back to the track, leaped, and made a snow-cone catch that turned into a double play and highlight-reel fodder for all-time. The Mets failed with the bases loaded in the bottom of the inning and, after Yadier Molina snapped the tie with a two-run blast that even Endy couldn't reach, the Mets left the bases loaded again in the ninth. Adam Wainwright's perfect curveball caught Beltran looking. It was like 1988 all over again. But this would prove more painful.

Those Season-Ending, Mind-Bending, Never-Ending Blues

The silver lining was that the core of the 2006 Mets would be together for a few years to come. The team that clubbed a club-record two hundred home runs in 2006 would hit .275 and steal two hundred bases in 2007, both club records.

But after leading the NL East for 159 days, the team came apart completely. Hitting, pitching, and defense failed them—and they could not right themselves. After being up by seven games with seventeen to play, the Mets finished 5–12, with two five-game losing streaks, and dropping five of six games to the Nationals. After winning three of four from the last-place Marlins the previous weekend, the Mets dropped two of three to Florida at home. The one win in that series came on the final Saturday, a game in which John Maine had a no-hitter until two were out in the eighth. With the Mets and Phillies tied in the standings, Tom Glavine, who had won his three-hundredth game two months earlier, was knocked out of the game in the first inning, sealing the worst collapse in major league history.

The Mets, the second-oldest staff in the league, got hit harder and harder as the year progressed. In the final seventeen games, Mets starters had a 6.49 ERA, and the bullpen provided little relief at 5.27. Baseball business analyst Vince Gennaro estimated that the Mets left as much as $30 million "on the table" in lost playoff revenue as well as merchandise, tickets, and concessions. It all could have been avoided with just one more win against the Phillies, whom NL MVP Jimmy Rollins controversially (but presciently) declared in spring training to be "the team to beat."

The Mets couldn't beat the Phillies in 2008, either. The Mets stood 7½ games out of first place the week Randolph was replaced in mid-June. The Mets fired him in Los Angeles at 3 a.m., eastern time, after making him begin the team's fourth western swing in just over six weeks. Jerry Manuel, a former "Manager of the Year" with the White Sox, took over, and the Mets responded—some critics claimed that the turnaround was mostly due to some of the players' disconnect with Randolph. Carlos Delgado came alive after the managerial change, swatting twenty-four homers and knocking in sixty-seven from June 27 to September 10—better than anyone else in baseball in that span. Jose Reyes (116 runs, fifty-six steals, nineteen triples, and 204 hits) and David Wright (thirty-three HR, 124 RBI, .302/.390/.534 [batting average/on-base percentage/slugging percentage]) were superb. Carlos Beltran was at his finest, scoring 116 runs, knocking in 112 runs, and clubbing twenty-seven homers, including the final Mets home run at Shea Stadium.

No matter what the 2008 Mets did offensively—or how well new ace Johan Santana pitched on the mound—the one thing the Mets could count on was that the bullpen would blow it. Seven Johan Santana wins were squandered, and twenty-nine saves were blown all told. Billy Wagner blew seven saves before blowing out his elbow later in the year. The club's home of forty-four years ended its existence with a loss on the final day that put the Milwaukee Brewers in the postseason for the first time since 1982, when they were in the American League.

So Omar Minaya set about to right the wrongs from the previous year again. He imported new relievers to settle a bullpen . . . that wound up not pitching a significant game after July Fourth weekend in 2009. Just about everything went wrong with the Mets in the first season at their new home, including nightmare scenarios that occurred on the road—like Luis Castillo's dropped pop-up in the ninth at new Yankee Stadium that handed Francisco Rodriguez his first blown save as a Met. The Mets spiraled down the toilet from there, with the front office turning into a comedy act and the team becoming a tired show that few wanted to see. Some 3.16 million seats were sold at the new stadium, but many fans were letting the overpriced seats at Citi Field go to waste rather than waste a day watching a ninety-two-loss club that saw seventeen players go on the disabled list a total of twenty-two times.

Blaming injuries, ownership kept Minaya and Manuel on for 2010. The pair proved 2009 was no fluke.

Again the Mets contended for much of the first half and then fell off a cliff. The problem was that this team could not play on the road. And they lived up to the contention, going 32–49 away from Citi Field (believe it or not, a three-game improvement over 2009).

There were success stories like R. A. Dickey finding his knuckler at age thirty-five; Ike Davis, a rookie hurried to the majors, playing like a veteran with marvelous defense and poise, to go with seventeen homers, many of them moon shots; Jon Niese, likewise excelling in his first full season in the majors; and Mike Pelfrey, having one bad month in the middle of the year but surpassing expectations the rest of the year, with fifteen wins and 204 innings. Then there were the duds: Jason Bay, a $16 million-per-year signee who hit six home runs before hitting a wall and missing the second half with a concussion; K-Rod, who was already having a lousy season before tearing a thumb ligament after fighting the grandfather of his children on Citi Field property; and the grossly underachiever twins, Luis Castillo (.604 OPS) and Oliver Perez (no wins and 6.80 ERA).

The Mets flitted between a game under and a game over .500 for well over a month before finally settling on finishing under .500, the last push coming on the final walk of Oliver Perez's Mets career in the fourteenth inning of a cruel season ender. At least it was shorter than it was back in April, when the Mets won their first twenty-or-more-inning game in five tries.

Expectations were reduced even further in 2011. Minaya was replaced by esteemed baseball veteran Sandy Alderson, who brought along former GMs Paul DePodesta and J. P. Ricciardi. The mission was to build a winner, not simply buy one—a formula that had never worked for the Mets anyway. Terry Collins, who'd been minor league field coordinator in 2010, was hired as the twentieth manager in franchise history. Ownership's role—and finances—became a serious issue when the lawyer overseeing the restitution for the Bernie Madoff Ponzi scheme called out the Wilpons as not simply victims but as having "benefited from Madoff's fraud." Even as the Mets identified a new minority owner in financier David Einhorn (a deal that eventually fizzled), opinion of ownership continued to drop when Fred Wilpon denigrated several of his stars in a *New Yorker* article and summed up the team's travails with a cavalier, "We're snakebitten, baby."

Speak for yourself. The Mets have been around for half a century. They have survived a 120-loss birth, M. Donald Grant, Mettle the Mule, two prolonged strikes, two years of Art Howe, and season-ending collapses you wouldn't wish on an enemy. Mets fans are built tough, yet soft enough on the inside to still carry around pieces of 1969, 1973, 1984, 1986, 1988, 1997, 1999, 2000, 2006, and many other seasons that are significant to those who lived through them or just lived through them vicariously in books or episodes of *Mets Yearbook* on the team's station, SNY. The Mets identity is forever changing, but the logo is still the same and so is the chant. "Let's go Mets." Let's.

Best Mets Players

IRST, A FEW WORDS ON METHODOLOGY: Coming up with the fifty greatest Mets is a lot easier than ranking them. The rankings in this chapter, however, are based on Mets influence, legacy, traditional and untraditional statistics, and longevity. I've done lists like this before, but things change. Even with players who've been retired for a while, their accomplishments can be amplified or reduced when compared to those who followed them.

Among the many numbers looked at was Wins Above Replacement (WAR), the latest in a long line of statistics purporting to accurately measure ballplayers from different eras. Two lists of players based on WAR are provided later in this chapter, as are lists of top fives as chosen by some of the Mets on this list—and a list from a newspaper in 2011.

There are certain players who don't get a fair shake from WAR, however, especially relief pitchers. Likewise, pitchers from eras of great pitching tend to have higher numbers than do pitchers who pitched during more-offensive periods; similarly, hitters from pitching-dominant eras are often lapped by more-recent players who regularly put up numbers only dreamed of by Mets of the 1960s and 1970s. There has yet to be a formula that adequately takes into account historical significance. In these rankings you get extra points for being Mookie Wilson, Jesse Orosco, Rusty Staub, Ed Kranepool, and Tug McGraw. Read on for why.

Asterisks indicate the player is a member of the Mets Hall of Fame.

☙ The Best Fifty Mets ☙

1. Tom Seaver,* RHP (1967–1977, 1983)

When it comes to a list of greatest Mets, there is one given: start with Seaver and everyone else slots in. The Mets landed Seaver by luck, winning the rights to him in 1966 after a technicality voided his signing with the Braves. He was NL Rookie of the Year a year later, winning sixteen games in each of his first two years—for a struggling team. When the Mets were suddenly ready to win in 1969, Seaver led the way. He won twenty-five games, came within two outs of a perfect game, captured the first postseason win in franchise history, and after a rocky World Series debut, threw ten innings of one-run ball. Seaver was *Sports Illustrated*'s Sportsman of the Year and won the first of his three Cy Young Awards. He could have won another in 1971, when he had his second twenty-win season and recorded league and career highs with 289 strikeouts and 1.76 ERA. (Twenty-four-game winner Ferguson Jenkins of the Cubs claimed that year's Cy Young.)

As the Mets rallied from last place to first in the final month of the 1973 season, Seaver won the NL East clincher, the NLCS clincher, and had a chance to do the same in the World Series on short rest, but Oakland wound up as world champions. "The Franchise" rebounded from an off year in 1974 to claim his third Cy Young in 1975, while also setting the major league mark with eight straight 200-strikeout seasons. The coming of free agency and escalating salaries created tension between Seaver and Mets Chairman M. Donald Grant, resulting in the heartbreaking trade to Cincinnati in 1977 that signaled the decline of the team as surely as Seaver's arrival in Flushing had indicated a change in the team's previously miserable fortunes. "Miserable" sums up the Mets during Seaver's exile, but he returned for the 1983 season. His Opening Day homecoming was the most joyous occasion at Shea Stadium since his departure, but the team still had a ways to go. Hindered by the same lack of support he'd endured in his first tenure, Seaver netted just a 9–14 mark despite leading the team in ERA, strikeouts, and innings. Though he was lost to the White Sox the following winter because of a player compensation miscalculation—resulting in him claiming win number 300 at Yankee Stadium in 1985 while pitching for Chicago—Seaver's numbers were already cemented atop the club record book.

Seaver is the team's all-time leader by a vast margin in wins (198), ERA (2.57), strikeouts (2,541), innings (3,045), shutouts (44), and starts (395), among other categories. Number 41 was the first—and only—number retired for a Mets player in 1988, the same year he was inducted into the Mets Hall of Fame. Four years later, he received 98.8 percent of the vote in Cooperstown, the highest Hall of Fame percentage in history. His ranking by Baseball-Reference.com as the game's sixth-best pitcher doesn't seem high enough (B-R calculates his Wins Above Replacement as fourth best all-time among pitchers), yet Seaver is without question number one when it comes to the Mets. And may it always be so.

2. Dwight Gooden,* RHP (1984–1994)

Doc Gooden burst onto the scene like no Met in history. Neither Tom Seaver nor Jerry Koosman approached Gooden's first two years in the majors. Gooden joined the Mets in 1984 at age nineteen, a secret weapon that continued to baffle the National League long after the secret was out. He fanned a rookie record and major league–best 276, including consecutive outings whiffing sixteen. His walks and hits per inning rate of 1.073 was also tops in the majors. Just as the Mets would have won the division if not for a remarkable year by the Cubs, Gooden (17–9, 2.60 ERA) would have won the Cy Young if not for 16–1 Chicago pickup Rick Sutcliffe. Gooden was otherworldly in 1985. Dr. K won the pitching Triple Crown (twenty-four wins, 1.53 ERA, and 268 K's), the only Met ever to do so, while also leading the league with sixteen complete games and 276.2 innings with a WHIP (walks plus hits per inning pitched) of 0.965. His adjusted ERA of 229 was the best of any pitcher between 1968 and 1994. Gooden did not lose between May 25 and August 30, 1985, becoming—at twenty—the youngest twenty-game winner ever. During that final month, he went nine innings in five of six games (he threw a mere eight innings in a 12–1 laugher). The Mets finished an agonizingly close second, though Gooden captured every first-place vote to become the first Met other than Seaver to claim the Cy Young.

He was a mere mortal in 1986, though his team was not. Gooden had 17 of the Mets' 108 victories and was superb in the NLCS, allowing just two runs over seventeen innings, including ten innings of one-run ball in Game 5. He lost both World Series starts and lost almost the first two months of the 1987 season to cocaine rehabilitation. He still won fifteen of his twenty-five starts and finished fifth in the Cy Young voting. In 1988, Gooden started—and lost—his second All-Star Game. After entering June 1990 with a 3–5 mark and an ERA hovering around 4.50, Gooden won sixteen of his last eighteen decisions, failing to get his twentieth win in his final start. That was Doc's last superlative year, though he remained the team's ace and face. That ended when he failed several drug tests in 1994 and was suspended for a year. Gooden enjoyed some later success with the Yankees, including a no-hitter. In Mets annals, Doc remains second to Seaver in wins (157) and strikeouts (1,875); he stands third—behind Seaver and Koosman—in starts (303), complete games (67), losses (85), innings (2,169.2), hits (1,898), and walks (651); and he is fourth in shutouts (23). He was inducted into the Mets Hall of Fame in 2010.

3. Darryl Strawberry,* OF (1983–1990)

Strawberry could exasperate management, teammates, and fans, but no Mets hitter has equaled his output. Like Dwight Gooden, the most frustrating part is how much better he might have been without alcohol and drugs clouding much of his career. On the field, Straw's numbers speak volumes. David Wright, playing more games as a Met, will likely surpass most of Strawberry's marks—as Straw passed many of the records set by Ed Kranepool, who was a Met a decade longer than was Strawberry. Straw's records include most home runs (252), multihomer games (22), RBI (733), extra-base hits (469), runs (662), and walks (580). His slugging percentage mark of .520 was surpassed by Mike Piazza. Records that nobody can catch are the most home runs at Shea Stadium in a season (24 in 1990) and career (127), plus the all-time Shea records for RBI (388) and runs (324).

Yet, Strawberry left Shea after contentious contract talks following a 1990 season that was among his best: 37 homers and a career-best 108 RBI despite not having the kind of lineup protection he'd enjoyed in the past. Strawberry returned to his native Los Angeles and a spiral of injury and addiction problems dogged him. He played in two World Series for the Yankees in the 1990s, but his lone World Series home run came in clinching Game 7 for the 1986 Mets. The first pick in the nation in the 1980 draft, Straw was 1983 National League Rookie of the Year. He finished in the top six in MVP voting three times as a Met. He led the NL in homers, slugging, and OPS (on-base plus slugging) in 1988. Strawberry and Howard Johnson were the first teammates in history to each hit 30 homers and steal 30 bases in the same year in 1987 (Straw missed reaching 30-30 again by one steal in 1988). Straw was voted the NL's All-Star starting right fielder in his last seven seasons as a Met; he missed the 1989 game with an injury but he hit .333 while representing New York as an All-Star. Strawberry was inducted into the Mets Hall of Fame in 2010.

4. Mike Piazza, C (1998–2005)

Piazza may have put up better numbers in the Los Angeles portion of his career, but he had more impact in New York as the rock in the Mets lineup from the moment he arrived on Memorial Day weekend in 1998. Famously drafted by the Dodgers in the sixty-second round at the request of his godfather Tommy Lasorda, Piazza actually became a Met from the Marlins, who'd pulled off a blockbuster trade with L.A. a week earlier. Piazza turned Shea into his playground, blasting balls to right field like a left-handed hitter, and pulling balls to distant areas of left field. He was inexplicably booed briefly in the weeks after the trade, but the cheers quickly drowned that out as he produced a staggering line of .348/.417/.607 with 23 homers and 76 RBI in his first 109 games as a Met. Given a seven-year contract to stay, Piazza hit 33 or more home runs for four straight seasons and his 220 homers are second in Mets history to Darryl Strawberry's 255. Piazza's .542 slugging is tops in franchise history, while his .295 average, 655 RBI, 415 extra-base hits, 193 doubles, and .373 on-base percentage are all among the best in team annals. Piazza started behind the plate in six All-Star Games as a Met, plus he missed another year after being drilled in the head by Roger Clemens; that soap opera culminated with Piazza drilling a ball to the back of the bullpen off Clemens at Shea in 2002.

One of the most popular Mets ever, fans even forgave Piazza's unsightly play after shifting to first base in 2004. He returned to catcher, where he collected a major league record 396 career homers, and exited to thunderous applause in his final game as a Met in 2005. After playing with San Diego and Oakland, he retired in 2008. He retired Shea Stadium later that year, catching the last pitch from Tom Seaver after the ballpark's final game. He caught Seaver's first pitch at Citi Field the following April.

5. Jerry Koosman,* LHP (1967–1978)

Though often overlooked next to Tom Seaver, Koosman gave the Mets half of a dynamic duo that National League clubs dreaded for almost a decade. Drafted into the army in 1962, Koosman considered becoming a helicopter pilot, but his dentist—a general in the Minnesota National Guard—helped him transfer to where he could pitch. A Shea Stadium usher's son stationed with Kooz passed along a recommendation, and the Mets signed him. The southpaw struggled and the Mets planned to release Koosman in early 1966, but they did not because he owed the team money following a car accident on the way to spring training. Koosman mastered the slider and paid the club back in spades. As a rookie, he tossed back-to-back shutouts to start the 1968 season. An All-Star—the rookie got the save for the National League—Kooz won nineteen times for a ninth-place team. For the Mets of that era, ninth place was an improvement. Kooz improved, and so did his team. Despite having arm problems early in 1969, he won seventeen times, completing sixteen of them, and tossed six shutouts—giving him thirteen in his first two seasons—as the Mets rallied to take the NL East. After Seaver dropped the World Series opener, Kooz held the Orioles hitless until the seventh inning of Game 2 and pulled out the 2–1 victory. He gave up two early home runs and nothing else in Game 5, with Davey Johnson's fly to left off Kooz clinching the world championship.

Koosman—and the Mets—had trouble coming up with an encore. Injuries prevented him from making thirty starts in any of the next three seasons, but he bounced back in 1973 with a club record 31.2 consecutive shutout innings as the Mets surged to the division title. He registered double-digit complete games each of the next four seasons, culminating with his lone twenty-win season as a Met. (Just as happened with the 1968 NL Rookie of the Year, Kooz finished a close second for the 1976 Cy Young.) But the Mets soon fell to pieces, trading Seaver and sticking Koosman with twenty losses in 1977 and a 3–15 mark in 1978, giving him the most career defeats by a Met (137). The Mets acquiesced to his wishes and traded him home to Minnesota—getting Jesse Orosco in the process—and Koosman won twenty as a Twin in 1979. He retired in 1985 and was elected to the Mets Hall of Fame in 1989, a year after Seaver.

Kooz's Top Five

1. Tom Seaver
2. Dwight Gooden
3. Jerry Grote
4. Bud Harrelson
5. Jerry Koosman

6. David Wright, 3B (2004–2011)

Wright spent much time learning from former Mets coach Howard Johnson, and, in some ways, these Mets third basemen from different decades are mirror images. Both showed prodigious power and could be erratic in the field. Both struck out frequently and had enough speed to rack up high steal totals. But chances are Wright will surpass Johnson and every other Met—save perhaps for steals and triples, the property of Jose Reyes, the man who teamed with Wright to forge the best left side of the infield in club history. Like Reyes, Wright jumped to the majors ahead of schedule during the Art Howe regime and barely needed a breaking-in period. At age twenty-one, Wright homered fourteen times and knocked in forty runs in sixty-nine games in 2004. His .293 average turned out to be his lowest until 2010. In each of the next four seasons, Wright posted at least twenty-six homers, 102 RBI, ninety-six runs, forty doubles, and fifteen steals.

Chosen with the compensation pick the Mets received when Mike Hampton became a free agent in 2000, Wright has won two Silver Sluggers and two Gold Gloves, though his defense can be erratic. Wright joined HoJo (and Darryl Strawberry) as Mets in the 30-30 club in 2007, and was thirty-four of thirty-nine in steal attempts while adding ninety-four walks. The following year he drove in 124 runs, though he knocked home no one in the final series of the year at home against Florida as the Mets were nudged out of a postseason berth by one game—again. Wright responded to spacious Citi Field in 2009 with his lowest home run output since he was in the Appalachian League in 2001. Wright's power numbers rebounded in 2010, with twenty-nine homers and 102 RBI. His average, however, dipped to .283, he set the club record for strikeouts, and led the National League in

"You've Gotta Have Heart"

There's something about being a Mets fan that makes one crave the underdog. That's why many are Mets fans in the first place. The Mets of the early days were especially filled with underdog players. Here's a handful that stand out when it comes to fan love.

Marv Throneberry (1962–1963)

The 1962 Mets became the first major league team to surpass two hundred errors since World War II, and nobody made errors with the panache of Marv Throneberry. "Marvelous Marv" was acquired to fill in for injured Gil Hodges, and he provided plenty of laughs, from missing first—and second—on a triple to committing seventeen errors in ninety-seven games at first base. And Throneberry famously got the last word in many a Lite Beer commercial. He could thank the Mets for making those residual checks possible.

Rod Kanehl (1962–1964)

"Hot Rod" Kanehl didn't hit (.241 career average), walk (.277 on-base percentage), or field (thirty-two errors at seven positions in 1962), but early Mets fans looked beyond—way beyond—the numbers. Here was a hustling kid stuck in the Yankees farm system, who got a chance when expansion rolled around. A game-tying hit against Sandy Koufax in a spring training game televised back to New York got people's attention, and once he made the club, he kept fans on the edge of their seats. Kanehl scored from second on a wild pitch to give the Mets their first win at the Polo Grounds. He also clubbed the first Mets grand slam. At six foot one, he wasn't small, but Mets fans still thought of Hot Rod as the little Met that could.

George Theodore (1973–1974)

> *"I'm not a gifted athlete, so I just have to perform up to what I think I can."*

Bespectacled, curly haired Theodore had a gait and an overall manner reminiscent of a stork. He was a fan's ballplayer—the kind of player someone in the stands could envision themselves being . . . if they had baseball talent. "The Stork" had just enough. Taken in the thirty-first round of the 1969 draft out of the University of Utah, he possessed a mixture of candor and originality rare in a ballplayer. He admitted, "I'm not a gifted athlete, so I just have to perform up to what I think I can." Injuries to others in 1973 gave him a shot in the lineup and he batted in the .290s in May. A frightening July collision with Don Hahn broke his hip. He returned in the fall and batted twice in the World Series, but a .158 average in 1974 relegated The Stork to minor legend.

Benny Agbayani (1998–2001)

A quarter century after The Stork, there came the next true fan legend: Benny Agbayani. Like fellow Hawaiian Sid Fernandez, Agbayani wore number 50—and he responded with ten homers in his first seventy-three at bats. He saw even more time in 2000 after Rickey Henderson's release, putting together a .289/.391/.477 line in 414 plate appearances. His homer into the teeth of the wind in the thirteenth inning won Game 3 of the 2000 NLDS. Traded to Colorado, he never found a home in the majors outside of Shea. He followed Bobby Valentine to Japan and played for the Chiba Lotte Marines.

Turk Wendell (1997–2001)

By the time the Mets got Turk from the Cubs in 1997, his chewing black licorice and brushing his teeth between innings had faded to acceptable levels of candy desire and dental hygiene. He just wanted the ball. And Bobby Valentine gave it to him. In 1998, Wendell pitched in nine straight games in September. The following year he became the first Met to pitch eighty times in a season, getting eight outs in his last appearance in a must-win game on the final day. Two days later, Turk won the first Mets postseason game since 1988—and his three postseason victories tie him for second on the all-time Mets list. Wendell was one of the few non-closing relievers to be worthy of a merchandised numbered tee shirt. Number 99 did it all with an everyman approach and a rosin-bag slam that woke the echoes at Shea Stadium.

both total chances and errors at third base. He endured his longest drought in the majors (0 for 20) in 2011 and then hit three home runs in the next four games. It was later revealed he was playing with a stress fracture in his back and he returned to the lineup just as Carlos Beltran was traded in late July. Through good times and bad, Wright has been the face of the franchise.

7. Keith Hernandez,* 1B (1983–1989)

The day Keith Hernandez arrived in New York, June 15, 1983, the Mets franchise changed. In Hernandez, they had an All-Star who'd won a batting title, was the game's top defender at first base, shared an NL MVP Award, and coolly knocked in the tying runs in the sixth inning of the seventh game of the World Series the previous October . . . on his twenty-ninth birthday. Though, initially, he was not sure that he wanted to remain a Met, Hernandez soon formed friendships and became the leader on the field and in the clubhouse. A talented core of young players quickly filled in around him. The Mets, who had not played better than .420 ball in seven years, won ninety games in 1984. Hernandez hit .311 with fifteen homers, ninety-four RBI, and ninety-seven walks, finishing second in the MVP balloting. He hit .309 the next year and .310 in 1986, placing fourth and eighth in the MVP voting, respectively.

"Mex," as he was called—though the San Franciscan's ancestors came from Spain—helped the Mets cakewalk to the '86 division title after two near misses. He scored the tying run in the ninth inning of epic Game 6 of the NLCS and, seven innings later, aggressively went for a force play that turned out to be the difference in the 7–6, sixteen-inning clincher at the Astrodome. His biggest hit knocked in two runs in the sixth inning of Game 7 of the 1986 World Series, breaking up lefty Bruce Hurst's shutout as the Mets went on to beat Boston. He was named the first captain in Mets history the following season. In 1988, he made up for an injury-plagued season by driving in five runs in the NLCS, though the Dodgers knocked off the Mets. With his legs ailing and his contract expiring—he played so sparingly in 1989 that he was not awarded a Gold Glove for the first time since 1978—Hernandez signed a two-year deal with Cleveland and, due to injuries, appeared in just forty-three games. Hernandez returned to the Mets in 1999 as an outspoken and beloved broadcaster.

Keith's Top Five

1. Tom Seaver
2. Darryl Strawberry
3. Dwight Gooden
4. Mike Piazza
5. David Wright

8. Jose Reyes, SS (2003–2011)

"Jose! Jose! Jose! Jose!" Shea Stadium rang with this chant as fans, teammates, and opponents sensed something was about to happen. When Reyes joined the Mets on the eve of his twentieth birthday in 2003, he quickly became the team's most exciting player since Mookie Wilson. The Mets were a different team with the remarkably skilled and exuberant shortstop at the top of the lineup. Leg injuries derailed his first two seasons as a Met and the front office converted him to a second baseman for a season before wisely switching him back to shortstop in 2005. That season, Reyes came to the plate more than any other player in baseball and finished atop the National League in steals and triples. He led the NL in both categories three times and shattered those franchise career marks as well by age twenty-five. He averaged 158 games for four straight seasons and became the second Met in history with two hundred hits in a season in 2008. He batted .300 in 2006, enjoying perhaps his best season: nineteen homers, eighty-one RBI, 122 runs, and sixty-four steals for the division champions, while placing sixth in the MVP balloting. He batted .281 and homered leading off must-win Game 6 of the NLCS against the Cardinals.

His failure—along with his team's—in the closing weeks of the 2007 and 2008 seasons overshadowed productive seasons (even if the free-swinging Jose's on-base percentage never did creep beyond the .350 range until 2011). Though his arm is among the game's best, his defense is sometimes erratic. His transfer to Citi Field, a ballpark seemingly built to showcase his talents, was far from the effortless transition that was envisioned as leg injuries essentially sapped a full season from Reyes over 2009 and 2010. Reyes claimed the first batting title in franchise history—albeit controversially, when he sat after one at bat in a tight race on the final day of 2011. It also marked the day his contract ran out.

9. Mookie Wilson,* OF (1980–1989)

MOOOOOOOOOOOOK! That is how the bottom of the first inning sounded at Shea Stadium for most of the 1980s. Mookie batted leadoff 681 times, including his first 258 starts as a Met. Mookie started more games in center field (907) than any Met before or since. Wilson had the most steals (281) and triples (62) of any Met in the franchise's first four decades, before Jose Reyes eclipsed him. William Hayward Wilson picked up his moniker as a child in South Carolina because he had trouble saying "milk," and Mookie became a catalyst in New York.

He scored ninety or more runs for the last-place 1982 and 1983 squads, ending two games in four days in 1983 by scoring from second base on balls that never left the infield. Though not a high average or on-base percentage kind of hitter, he did lead the 1982 and 1983 teams in those categories (which speaks of the team's offensive deficiencies at the time). A symbol of how far the Mets had come, Mookie fittingly was at the plate for perhaps the most pivotal at bat in Mets history in the tenth inning of Game 6 of the 1986 World Series—first jackknifing out of the way of a pitch to let the tying run score and then hitting the fabled ground ball toward Bill Buckner. Davey Johnson started platooning lefty-hitting Lenny Dykstra and playing the switch-hitting Wilson more in left field. Mookie remained an integral part of the team until he was shipped to Toronto in June 1989. He played in two more Championship Series for the Jays before retiring in 1991. Mookie returned to manage in the Mets system and served as New York's first-base coach under Bobby Valentine and, then, Terry Collins.

10. Cleon Jones,* OF (1963, 1965–1975)

Five decades after he was signed out of Mobile, Alabama, where he played high school ball with Tommie Agee, Jones remains one of the best outfielders the Mets organization has produced. It was the arrival of his friend Agee in 1968 that shifted Jones from center field to left. In 1969, Cleon was the National League's All-Star starting left fielder, collecting two hits and scoring twice while batting ahead of Johnny Bench. Jones hit .340 with a .433 on-base percentage for the season—both Mets high-water marks until surpassed by John Olerud in 1998.

When Gil Hodges walked out to left field in mid-inning and pulled Jones after he jogged after a ball in the summer of 1969, it seemed to spur the club. From that day on, the Mets played one hundred percentage points better than any NL club and two hundred points better than the Cubs, whom the Mets overtook in September. Jones batted .429 in the sweep of the Braves in the NLCS. He had just three hits in the World Series, but his greatest contribution came on a ball pitched near his shoe, as he was batting in Game 5. The ball skidded into the Mets dugout, and his manager brought out a smudged ball. Jones was sent to first, Donn Clendenon's homer followed, and the Mets took the lead two innings later. With two down in the ninth, Jones genuflected while catching the ball that made the Mets world champions. Left field at Shea Stadium saw another miraculous moment in the thirteenth inning on September 22, 1973, when a ball ticketed for the bullpen hit the top of the wall and bounced to Jones; his throw was relayed home and the tag applied at the plate. The Mets won the game and wound up going from last place to first in a month.

Jones batted .300 in the NLCS upset of the Reds and later hit a homer against the A's. Jones was again hit by a World Series pitch but no shoe polish or championship rubbed off. Injury and a controversy brought a sad end to Cleon's career as a Met, but he left the team in 1975 holding several career records, which were later surpassed by Ed Kranepool. Jones was inducted into the Mets Hall of Fame in 1991.

11. Edgardo Alfonzo, 2B-3B (1995–2002)

Alfonzo was forever coming up with the big hit in the middle of a rally. Defensively, he played where the Mets needed him (524 games at second base, 515 games at third) and fielded at a clip of .980 as a Met with just seventy-three errors in 3,752 chances. Manning the keystone on what *Sports Illustrated* postulated could be "The Best Infield Ever," Fonzie melded perfectly with slugging corner men John Olerud and Robin Ventura, while forming a magnificent double-play duo with Rey Ordonez. That year, he became the first Met to go six for six in a game, while setting club marks with six runs and sixteen total bases in a rout at the Astrodome. He hit a two-run homer in the first inning of a one-game playoff in Cincinnati and, the next night in Phoenix, tied Rusty Staub's 1973 club mark with five RBI in a postseason game, including a tiebreaking grand slam in the ninth.

The following year—his lone All-Star season—Fonzie hit .324, while surpassing one hundred runs, twenty-five home runs, and 90 RBI for the second straight year. He batted .444 in the 2000 NLCS to put the Mets in the World Series for the first time since 1986. Hampered by back problems in 2001, he returned to third base in 2002 and batted .308. The Mets let Fonzie go after the 2002 season, and he helped the Giants claim a division title and then batted .529 in the NLDS. He signed a minor league contract with the Mets in 2006, but Alfonzo never made it back to Flushing to add to his numbers that placed him in the top seven in Mets history in runs (614), RBI (538), total bases (1,736), hits (1,136), doubles (212), and multi-hit games (314), not to mention batting (.292) and on-base percentage (.367).

12. Carlos Beltran, OF (2005–2011)

The "New Mets" were born when Beltran took the podium after signing with the club in January 2005. That signing, which followed the arrival of Pedro Martinez weeks earlier, was supposed to signal a sea change in Mets fortunes. The team's profile increased significantly, but, at the same time, its failures became that much more epic. After a disappointing first season marked by injuries, Beltran put together three straight seasons where he *averaged* thirty-four home runs, 113 RBI, 112 runs, eighty-five walks, and twenty-two steals. The fleet center fielder also won Gold Glove Awards all three seasons and won Silver Sluggers in 2006 and 2007. He tied club marks in 2006 with forty-one homers and eighty extra-base hits, and set a Mets record with 127 runs to finish fourth in MVP voting. The price of signing the seven-year, $119 million outfielder weighed especially heavy when he made the last out of Game 7 in the 2006 NLCS, caught looking at an Adam Wainwright curve.

While the team struggled around him down the stretch the next two years, Beltran excelled in the final month of 2007 (eight homers, twenty-seven RBI, .282/.328/.596) and 2008 (six homers, nineteen RBI, .344/.440/.645). Beltran hit the last home run at Shea Stadium by a Met—a blast that briefly tied the do-or-die finale. He hit a career-best .325 in the first year at Citi Field in 2009, but he missed half of 2009 and 2010 with injuries, which necessitated a move to right field in 2011. His expiring contract necessitated a trade to a contender for the rebuilding-mode Mets. Beltran finished his Mets career with a bang, and he was tabbed by his future manager Bruce Bochy of the Giants as starting DH in the 2011 All-Star Game. Beltran ended his Mets career in the top seven in on base percentage (.369), slugging (.500), OPS (.869), doubles (208), home runs (149), and RBI (559).

13. Al Leiter, LHP (1998–2004)

Leiter grew up a Mets fan and turned into a Mets ace. The animated New Jersey southpaw was drafted by the Yankees—his brother Mark, a righty, was chosen by the Orioles and pitched eleven years in the majors. Al was a reliever for the 1993 champion Blue Jays and a starter for the 1997 champion Marlins. With Florida dismantling its team, the Mets grabbed Leiter (A. J. Burnett was one of three minor leaguers sent south in the deal). Leiter immediately established himself at the head of the Mets rotation, going 17–6 with a 2.47 ERA in 193 innings. The 1999 season did not go as well for Leiter, until his last start. With the Mets and Reds tied for the Wild Card on the season's final day, Leiter tossed a two-hit shutout in Cincinnati to put

Best-Hitting Pitchers

As proof that Tom Seaver doesn't head every Mets pitching category, here is a Seaver-free list of the top Mets hitting hurlers (Tom Terrific just missed making the top five). They are listed by adjusted on-base plus slugging (OPS+); their totals as Mets for home runs, RBI, and batting average/on base percentage/slugging are included as well, meager as they may seem. They are based on 150 or more plate appearances.

Table 1.1.   Best-Hitting Pitchers

	HR	RBI	AVG/OBP/SLG	OPS+
Rick Aguilera	3	11	.203/.236/.290	46
Dwight Gooden	7	65	.197/.213/.260	32
Ray Sadecki	0	9	.213/.236/.225	30
Tug McGraw	1	15	.172/.216/.229	26
Sid Fernandez	1	31	.190/.211/.232	25

the Mets in the postseason for the first time since 1988. He embarked on a string of stellar postseason outings that left him without a victory because Armando Benitez blew three of his would-be October wins over the next two seasons. Leiter stayed on the mound in his last postseason start until the game was decided on the 142nd pitch on a grounder up the middle by Luis Sojo in Game 5 of the World Series. One of just six Mets to make two hundred starts and the club's all-time leader with twenty-eight pickoffs, Leiter won fifteen times in 2003 for the team with the worst record in his seven seasons as a Met. He finished his career where he started it—as a Yankee—and joined their broadcast booth. A former postseason analyst for ESPN and Fox, Leiter also works for the MLB Network.

14. Tug McGraw,* LHP (1965–1967, 1969–1974)

Though Frank Edwin McGraw was the heart and soul of the 1973 "Ya Gotta Believe" Mets, his role with the 1969 Miracle Mets is often overlooked. His 0.84 ERA in the second half of 1969 covered forty-three innings, with seventeen games finished, seven saves, and only one home run allowed. McGraw pitched just once that postseason, thanks to the club's dominant starters. He posted successive seasons with an identical 1.70 ERA, got the win in the 1972 All-Star Game, and set the then–club mark with twenty-seven saves that same year. In the 1973 season, however, he looked as lost as he had in the mid-1960s as a struggling starter (his claim to fame under Casey Stengel was defeating Sandy Koufax, who'd been 13–0 against the Mets). McGraw's first 1973 win finally came on August 22, with the Mets still in last place. And from then on, there was no stopping Tug. His fourteen September appearances included three wins and ten saves, capped by the division clincher. He threw 13.2 innings of relief in the seven-game loss to Oakland in the World Series, tossing six innings in Game 2 to pick up the win. He was in pain the following year, and the Mets traded him rather than treat him or admit something might be wrong. After a simple procedure, his screwball was as good as new, and McGraw spent a decade with the Phillies. One of the great personalities in the game, he'd gotten his nickname as an eager infant at feeding time, and the Mets Hall of Fame southpaw lived up to that name. He died of a brain tumor at age fifty-nine in 2004. The Mets honored Tug by embroidering his 1973 saying on their sleeve: "Ya Gotta Believe."

15. Howard Johnson, 3B (1985–1993)

From his arrival in New York after taking part in Detroit's 1984 World Series victory, his name was shortened to the sobriquet of the then-popular ice cream parlor/restaurant/hotel chain. HoJo could be maddeningly inconsistent—especially in even-numbered years—but he fueled the Mets with both speed and power at the hot corner, and he was versatile enough to also play shortstop and the outfield. Three times (1987, 1989, 1991) he finished in the top ten in the MVP balloting, while also making the 30-30 club. (In 1987, HoJo and Darryl Strawberry became the first teammates in history to each have thirty homers and thirty steals in the same year.) Johnson led the National League with 104 runs in 1989 and, two years later, became the first Met to lead the league in homers and RBI. On leaving the team after the 1993 season, he stood second in club history in home runs (192), RBI (629), runs (627), doubles (214), extra-base hits (424), and steals (202). He later served in the organization as a minor league manager and as batting coach in New York.

16. Gary Carter,* C (1985–1989)

"Kid" Carter was a Hall of Fame catcher whose greatest seasons came as an Expo, but his greatest moments came as a Met. New York sent four players to Montreal for the perennial All-Star in December 1984. His first year, he became the first Met to hit thirty home runs and drive in one hundred runs in the same season. He had 105 RBI the following season and placed third in the MVP voting behind Mike Schmidt as the Mets ran away with the NL East. Locked in a one-for-twenty-one slump in the playoffs, Carter knocked in the winning run in the twelfth inning in Game 5 against Houston. His greatest extra-inning feat as a Met, though, was starting the miraculous rally against Boston in the tenth inning of Game 6 in the World Series. He drove in nine runs in the Series and was the first to engulf Jesse Orosco after the final out in Game 7. After enduring years of physical punishment as the National League's premier signal caller for a decade, his body wore down. Carter managed his ninth twenty-homer year in 1987, but he hit just .235. The following year, he joined Keith Hernandez as Mets cocaptain, collected his three-hundredth homer (following two homerless months), and was an All-Star for the eleventh—and final—time. He left the Mets after the 1989 season, as did Hernandez. Carter was inducted into the Mets Hall of Fame in 2001 and into Cooperstown two years later.

17. David Cone, RHP (1987–1991, 2003)

Coney came to the Mets from Kansas City in one of the great heists in Mets history and, due to injuries, landed in the rotation as a rookie in 1987. He stayed in the rotation until he was injured trying to bunt. His second year was magnificent despite beginning the year in the bullpen. He went 20–3 with a 2.22 ERA, 213 strikeouts, .213 opponent batting average, and league-best .293 opponent slugging and .870 winning percentage. With the Mets needing to win at Dodger Stadium to push the NLCS to a seventh game, Cone went the distance. Too bad he couldn't pitch Game 7, too. Cone won fourteen games in each of the next three seasons, although his team's fortunes slipped. He led the league in strikeouts in 1990 and 1991, including nineteen on the final day of the latter season. He had thirteen wins, an NL-best five shutouts, and a league-high 214 strikeouts when he was traded to the Blue Jays in late August. Cone missed claiming the NL strikeout crown at the end of the year by one K. He won the 1994 American League Cy Young with his hometown Royals before being shipped to the Blue Jays and then the Yankees. He played in four World Series as a Yankee, including against the Mets in 2000, and tossed a perfect game in 1999. He retired with the Red Sox in 2001 before rejoining the Mets to pick up one final win at age forty in 2003. He later became a Yankees broadcaster.

18. Jesse Orosco, LHP (1979, 1981–1987)

Orosco broke Tug McGraw's single-season and career club saves marks, and John Franco topped Orosco's records, but of those three great southpaw relievers in Mets history, none threw a glove like Messy Jesse. Orosco was from the McGraw mold, tossing multiple innings in six of his eight appearances in the 1986 postseason. Three of those innings came in epic Game 6 of the NLCS at the Astrodome, clinching the pennant on fumes as he tossed his fifth frame of extra-inning relief in just over twenty-four hours. He earned three of the four wins against Houston and saved two World Series wins against Boston, most notably Game 7, when he sent his glove airborne after fanning Marty Barrett with his 188th postseason pitch of 1986. Traded by

Best-Pitching Hitters

The Mets have been blown out of many a game during their half century of existence. Only a handful of times, though, has it gotten to the point where a fielder has been called in to finish things up on the mound. It took thirty seasons before the first, Bill Pecota, toed the rubber on September 26, 1992. Matt Franco, called on after an injury to a real pitcher in his 1999 mound debut, is the lone Mets position player to take the hill more than once in a career—or a season.

Table 1.2. Best-Pitching Hitters

	H	HR	BB	SO	ERA	Year	Score[a]
Desi Relaford	0	0	0	1	0.00	2001	15–3
Bill Pecota	1	1	0	0	9.00	1992	19–2
Matt Franco	3	1	3	2	13.50	1999	16–0, 14–3[b]
Derek Bell	1	0	3	0	36.00	2000	16–1
Todd Zeile	4	0	2	0	45.00	2004	19–10

[a] Score reflects the final score *after* the carnage was complete.
[b] Matt Franco pitched on July 2 *and* August 8, 1999.

the Twins in 1979 for Jerry Koosman—ironically, the lefty who'd been on the hill when the Mets clinched the 1969 world championship—Orosco burst on the scene in 1983. The All-Star's thirteen wins, seventeen saves, 1.47 ERA, and third-place Cy Young standing belied his club's last-place finish. He saved a then–club-record thirty-one games the following year for a rejuvenated contender. He later alternated with Roger McDowell in the bullpen—and in a memorable 1986 contest, between the outfield and the mound. His 2.73 ERA is tops for a lefty with 500 innings. Traded to the Dodgers after the 1987 season, Orosco pitched until age forty-six, in 2003, retiring with the all-time major league appearance record of 1,252.

19. Sid Fernandez, LHP (1984–1993)

Similar to Jon Matlack of a decade earlier, Fernandez wasn't flashy, but opposing batters knew they were in for a tough time against this lefty. El

Sid allowed just 6.85 hits per nine innings for his career, third-lowest in history behind only Nolan Ryan and Sandy Koufax. Despite his wildness, the big guy from the Aloha State still managed twenty-three complete games as a Met, including nine shutouts. Yet, his lasting contribution to Mets history was a relief outing during Game 7 of the 1986 World Series. Ron Darling got knocked out in the fourth inning with the Mets trailing Boston, 3–0; Fernandez entered, walked batting champ Wade Boggs, and then set down the next eight batters he faced. The Mets fought back to win the game and the title. Fernandez had gaudy marks of 16–6 in 1986 and 14–5 with a league-best .737 winning percentage in 1989. He won fourteen times for the "Worst Team Money Could Buy" in 1992 and had a presentable 5–6 mark with a 2.93 ERA during an injury-plagued 1993 season for a 103-loss club. It was his final year as a Met, leaving just two wins shy of one hundred, with a 3.14 ERA as a Met. He is fourth in club history in starts (250) and strikeouts (1,449), and fifth in innings (1,584.2) and walks (596).

20. Jon Matlack, LHP (1971–1977)

Matlack was often seen as the third wheel behind Tom Seaver and Jerry Koosman in a stacked Mets rotation, but the southpaw was superb in his own right. The fourth overall pick in the 1967 draft, Matlack took Nolan Ryan's spot in the rotation following the disastrous deal with the Angels—but Jon certainly took a little of the immediate sting away by earning 1972 Rookie of the Year. A year later, a line drive fractured his skull, yet he was back throwing a one-hitter less than a month later. He tossed a two-hit shutout in Cincinnati in the NLCS after the Mets had lost the opener in the ninth inning the previous day. He started three games in that year's World Series, going 1–2 despite a 2.16 ERA. Matlack was an All-Star three times, getting the win and sharing MVP honors with Bill Madlock in 1975. He finished in the top ten in the league in strikeouts in each of his first five seasons as a Met and twice led the National League in shutouts. His twenty-six shutouts are tied with Koosman for most by a Met not named Seaver. He is also in the top ten in starts (199), complete games (65), wins (82), losses (81), innings (1,448), strikeouts (1,043), and his 3.03 ERA is second to Seaver among Mets starters with at least 1,000 innings.

21. Ron Darling, RHP (1983–1991)

Though often in the shadow of fellow 1984 rookie Dwight Gooden, Darling held his own and was one of the reasons the Mets had the most feared rotation in the National League for the last half of the 1980s. He struggled with control, especially early in his career—leading the league in bases on balls in 1985 and coming within two of Nolan Ryan's 1971 club mark of 116 walks. Yet Darling put together 16-6 and 15-6 seasons in 1985 and 1986 with a sub-3.00 ERA both years. In 1986, he joined Jon Matlack (1973) as the only Met to start three times in a World Series, winning Game 4 at his hometown Fenway Park. Darling clinched the 1988 division title at Shea with a complete game—one of seven times he went the distance that year—and he won a career-best seventeen times. He finished one win shy of one hundred as a Met and recorded six straight two-hundred-inning seasons. Fifteen years after the Mets traded him, Darling returned to the team's broadcast booth with Gary Cohen and former teammate Keith Hernandez in 2006.

22. Bud Harrelson,* SS (1965–1977)

Harrelson was never much of a hitter—as his .236 average and .288 slugging attest—but his defense and speed were critical for a team that depended on great pitching. Though often injured, Harrelson had staying power with the Mets. Only teammate Ed Kranepool surpassed Harrelson's franchise marks for games (1,322) and at bats (4,390). He stood as the club's career leader in stolen bases (115) and triples (45) when he was traded in 1978. A Gold Glove winner and two-time All-Star, he served as Mets announcer, coach, and manager after retiring, but he is still best known for getting into a fight with Pete Rose during the 1973 NLCS. He lost the bout, but the Mets won the pennant.

Buddy's Top Five

1. Tom Seaver
2. Dwight Gooden
3. Darryl Strawberry
4. Ed Kranepool
5. Cleon Jones

23. Jerry Grote,* C (1966–1977)

Gruff Grote was the drill sergeant who broke in the great Mets pitching staff of the late 1960s and early 1970s. And what a staff it was. Tom Seaver, Jerry Koosman, and Nolan Ryan, as well as Gary Gentry, Jon Matlack, and Craig Swan all started their careers throwing to Grote. He played in the same era as Reds superstar Johnny Bench and never won a Gold Glove because of it, but Grote's old-style catching technique—complete with cap turned around and bill flipped up—along with his bullet arm intimidated many an opposing runner and a few raw Mets pitchers. Though Gil Hodges platooned at four different positions, catcher wasn't one of them. Grote played every inning of the postseason in both 1969 and 1973 and still holds the Mets record with twelve career hits in World Series play. He stands third in games played (1,235). He was traded shortly after Tom Seaver in 1977, just six hits shy of one thousand as a Met.

24. John Stearns, C (1975–1982, 1984)

Stearns was the heart and soul of a club that didn't seem to have much of either. Arriving in the Tug McGraw deal, he caught one of the league's top staffs in 1975, 1976, and half of 1977. He worked diligently with the pitchers that were left and guarded the plate like a knight-errant. The former University of Colorado defensive back also had surprising speed, setting a record for catchers with twenty-five steals in 1978—needless to say, he is the only backstop to ever lead the team in that category. Stearns was the team's lone representative in the All-Star Game in 1977, 1980, and 1982 (he had Lee Mazzilli for company in 1979). Injuries ended the career of "Bad Dude" just as the Mets were turning the corner.

Bad Dude's Top Five

1. Tom Seaver
2. Dwight Gooden
3. Darryl Strawberry
4. Mike Piazza
5. David Wright

25. Tommie Agee,* OF (1968–1972)

Soon after Gil Hodges was hired as manager in the fall of 1967, he set about trying to make Agee his center fielder. The Mets got him—and Al Weis—in a trade with the White Sox. Beaned in spring training, Agee was never right in 1968, but he turned his game—and his team—around in 1969. He started the year by becoming the only player to land a fair ball in the Shea upper deck, and he ended it with a home run in the first Shea World Series game while turning in two of the most Amazin' catches in club history. The team leader in runs (97), home runs (26), and RBI (76) out of the leadoff spot in 1969, he put up similar numbers in 1970 and became the first Met to win a Gold Glove. Injuries and the acquisition of Willie Mays brought about the end of the Agee era at Shea. He was posthumously inducted into the Mets Hall of Fame in 2002.

26. Lenny Dykstra (1985–1989)

The same size and temperament as Wally Backman, the combo at the top of the Mets order was known as "Backstra." He was also part of a platoon with Mookie Wilson in center field known as "Mookstra." Injuries to Wilson gave Dykstra his chance in 1985, and he mixed speed, bat control, and a masterful eye—plus he was a solid center fielder. Known as "Nails," Dykstra was plenty tough and came through at key moments; his home runs in Game 3 of the NLCS and World Series turned both series around. Trading him to the Phillies in 1989 started the change in the fortunes for both franchises. He had his problems holding onto his assets attained through finance during his retirement.

27. Lee Mazzilli (1979–1981, 1986–1989)

A Met during the team's nadir and pinnacle, Mazzilli was a Brooklyn heartthrob who started on Opening Day 1977 at age twenty-two and was a grizzled veteran off the bench for two Mets postseason teams in his thirties. Maz was a first-round pick in 1974, and he arrived in the majors as the Mets were dismantled. Not only was he the team's most marketable commodity—Lee Mazzilli Poster Day, anyone?—he was also the team's best player. Maz showed the world one night, homering and then driving in the go-ahead run with a walk in the 1979 All-Star Game. The team leader in almost every category, including home runs (16), RBI (76), and steals (41) in 1980, he was dealt after an injury-plagued 1981 season. He came back in 1986, was the key man off the bench that October, and stayed around until midway through 1989. A coach with the Yankees and a manager for the Orioles, charismatic Maz returned to the Mets for a few years on SNY.

28. Rusty Staub,* OF (1972–1975, 1981–1985)

When Staub arrived in a blockbuster deal with Montreal in 1972, he became the big man in a lineup lacking pop. A hand injury derailed a great start by Staub and his club in 1972, but the red-haired slugger returned to form the following year, helping the last-place Mets transform into division champions in an Amazin' September. Staub hit .307 and scored twenty-one runs in the final month and kept on hitting, collecting three home runs in the first three NLCS games before colliding with the wall and injuring his shoulder in the fourth game. He played all seven games against Oakland despite pain that forced him to throw underhand, yet he hit .423 while driving in six. Le Grande Orange became the first Met to surpass one hundred RBI in a season in 1975 and was promptly traded to Detroit by petty Mets president M. Donald Grant. (Staub would have gained the right to veto any trade once the 1976 season began.) Rusty returned to see the team rise up, becoming the game's premier pinch hitter. He tied major league marks with eight straight hits and twenty-five RBI as a pinch hitter in 1983. He played through the 1985 season, joined former teammate Bud Harrelson as the first players in the Mets Hall of Fame in 1986, and served as a broadcaster. An accomplished chef and philanthropist, Daniel Joseph Staub is still beloved in New York.

29. John Franco, LHP (1990–2001, 2003–2004)

Franco was born a Mets fan in Brooklyn and came home to New York from Cincinnati for Randy Myers in a straight-up deal of southpaw closers before the 1990 season. Myers won the World Series that year, but Franco stood the test of time. He saved 276 games as a Met and appeared on the

Best Mets in Postseason, All Series

When your team makes postseason appearances sporadically, at best, you remember who was a good October player, and who was not. These are the players you wanted up in the big moment.

Keep in mind the numbers below combine all levels of Mets postseason series through 2011, so the Division Series, Championship Series, and World Series are treated equally. Don't try this at home, kids.

Edgardo Alfonzo (1999, 2000 postseasons)

Alfonzo was an animal, sleek and quiet, and he was unstoppable in October. His twenty-four postseason games are tied with Robin Ventura for the most of any Met. Fonzie's twenty-six hits, seventeen RBI, fifteen runs, and eight doubles lead the pack. Oh, and in his first postseason game, he homered twice, including a tiebreaking grand slam in the ninth inning.

Jerry Koosman (1969, 1973 postseasons)

The Mets won all six starts Koosman made in his postseason career, including his two starts in the 1969 World Series. Jon Matlack's ERA was almost two runs better than Kooz's 3.38, and Tom Seaver threw more innings than Koosman's forty, but the big lefty had a way of doing what it took to win—and there's not much more you can ask for in the postseason.

Tug McGraw (1969, 1973 postseasons)

Tug McGraw, Armando Benitez, and Billy Wagner all had three saves in postseason play for the Mets. Which was more impressive? Tug pitched 20⅔ innings over three postseason series while Benitez threw 18 innings over fifteen appearances in five series. Tug pitched six innings in relief in Game 2 of the 1973 World Series.

Cleon Jones (1969, 1973 postseasons)

Second only to Edgardo Alfonzo in postseason hits (23), runs (14), and doubles (7), Cleon played every inning of every postseason game the Mets played in 1969 and 1973. He hit .429 in the 1969 NLCS and .300 against the Reds in 1973. Though he didn't hit much in the 1969 World Series, his shoe polish (supposedly) started the Game 5 comeback and his genuflecting catch sealed the Miracle.

Tom Seaver (1969, 1973 postseasons)

You simply can't have a list like this without Seaver. His 53⅔ innings and forty-six strikeouts are still tops in Mets October annals. He did lose three of his seven postseason starts, but his three wins were pretty impressive: the team's first postseason game in 1969, a ten-inning gem in Game 4 of that year's World Series, and the clincher in the 1973 NLCS.

Al Leiter (1999, 2000 postseasons)

Leiter persevered to get on this list. Like Seaver, he started seven games in the postseason. Though Leiter never got credit for a Mets postseason victory, he can thank Armando Benitez for blowing three wins for him. Leiter also lost a 1–0 game in the 1999 NLCS and the excruciating Game 5 defeat in the ninth inning of the 2000 World Series. His forty strikeouts and 45⅓ innings pitched are second to Seaver.

mound 695 times, both club records by a mile. His fourteen seasons as a Met are second only to Ed Kranepool. Franco led the National League in saves in 1990 and 1994 and retired in 2005 second on the all-time list with 426, the most saves by a southpaw. Though he missed all of 2002 because of Tommy John surgery, he made a comeback at age forty-two. Franco was the third captain in Mets history and the only one who was a pitcher.

30. John Olerud, 1B (1997–1999)

Many Mets have made significant marks with only three years of service, but no one has approached the three years put in by Olerud to cap the 1990s. He not only holds the team full season marks for batting (.354) and on-base percentage (.447), both set in 1998, Olerud also owns the career marks in those categories for Mets with at least two thousand plate appearances: .315 and .425, respectively. He averaged twenty-one homers, ninety-six runs, ninety-seven RBI, and 102 walks, and missed only ten games in his three seasons. The Mets missed him greatly when he left for his home in Seattle after the 1999 season.

31. Rick Reed, RHP (1997–2001)

Reed provided surprises throughout his four-plus seasons as a Met. Facing animosity from teammates for crossing the 1995 picket lines to help his ailing mother, Reed worked his way into the 1997 rotation and won thirteen times while finishing sixth in the league with a 2.87 ERA. He won sixteen times in 1998 and posted a .688 winning percentage in both 1999 and 2000. His three-hit shutout put the Mets into a tie for the Wild-Card lead on the penultimate day of the 1999 season. The Mets won his first starts in the NLDS, NLCS, and World Series, the latter against the Yankees in 2000. He twice was an All-Star Met.

32. Wally Backman, 2B (1980–1988)

The Mets may have lost Seaver in June 1977, but they gained Backman. Taken with the sixteenth overall pick in 1977, he went back and forth to the minors until Davey Johnson was promoted to manage New York in 1984. Johnson inserted Backman at second base and the second spot in the order but only against righties. A .294 career hitter left-handed, he batted just .165 from the right side, necessitating a platoon. That did, however, make Backman a late-game bench asset in games started by lefties. Two of his biggest contributions to the 1986 Mets came off the bench in the NLCS. He started the Game 3 rally as a pinch hitter with a drag bunt—and wide path to first—and knocked in a run and scored the run that turned out to be the difference in

Best Mets in Postseason, One Series

Earlier we looked at the best Mets when combining all the postseason stats. Now we look at the Mets who got the job done in one series. You start with the MVPs.

Al Weis (1969 World Series)

Weis won the Babe Ruth Award for the 1969 World Series (the Series MVP as chosen by the New York Baseball Writers). Weis got late key hits in both of Jerry Koosman starts, including his only career home run at Shea to tie Game 5 in the seventh inning. Feast your eyes on this line against the Orioles in the 1969 Series: .455/.563/.727. Good-field, no-hit Weis epitomized the success of a Gil Hodges platoon system that was simply Amazin' in 1969.

Donn Clendenon (1969 World Series)

Clendenon got the more prestigious *Sport* MVP Award and the sports car. He sat out Game 4 because of the platoon system. Clendenon clubbed three home runs and knocked in four, which is key when your club only scores fourteen runs in five games and still wins. The Mets pitchers deserved a ride in the Camaro Donn got from *Sport.*

Ray Knight (1986 World Series)

Knight batted .391 and knocked in five. His most important RBI was himself. His tiebreaking home run against Boston in the seventh inning of Game 7 led the Mets to a world championship and led him to the cover of *Sports Illustrated.* It couldn't jinx the already-won title, but it didn't help him. The Mets let Knight leave after the victory parade and gave the third-base job to the younger and more powerful Howard Johnson.

Mike Hampton (2000 NLCS)

He is the only Met to win an NLCS MVP. There was no MVP in the Championship Series in 1969 or 1973, and Jesse Orosco didn't get the 1986 NLCS MVP despite three wins (Houston's Mike Scott got the hardware, a consolation prize). Hampton deserved his award, not allowing a run in sixteen innings against the Cardinals, including a three-hit shutout in the pennant clincher at Shea. Like Ray Knight, he was not back in New York the following year, but the Colorado school systems made that happen.

Game 6. A five-foot-nine, down-and-dirty ballplayer, fans still love Wally, who was a finalist to manage the Mets in 2011 and was retained as a minor league skipper.

33. Ed Kranepool,* 1B-OF (1962–1979)

Longevity is Kranepool's legacy. The Bronx-bred Krane remains the longest-serving Mets player ever, debuting at age seventeen at the end of the club's inaugural 1962 season. He wore the uniform in each of the club's first eighteen seasons, through eight managers, five general managers, two World Series, and the building up and tearing down of the franchise. An All-Star at age twenty, Kranepool later platooned at first base for the 1969 champs, homering in Game 4 of the World Series. Just twenty-eight and transitioned to a bench role in 1973, he drove in the first two runs of New York's Game 5 NLCS clincher against the Reds. Steady Eddie led the league in pinch hitting in 1974 with a .486 average and is the club's all-time leader in pinch hits (90). He played his last game in 1979, retiring with most of the club's all-time offensive records, including games (1,853), at bats (5,436), and hits (1,418).

Steady Eddie's Top Five

1. Tom Seaver
2 Mike Piazza
3. Jerry Koosman
4. Ed Kranepool
5. Jose Reyes
5. David Wright (tie)

34. Kevin McReynolds, LF (1987–1991, 1993)

Not always remembered fondly around Flushing, Kevin Mac put up impressive numbers. The Mets traded Kevin Mitchell, a rookie World Series hero—and future NL MVP with the Giants—to bring McReynolds to Shea for the 1987 season. His stellar 1988—twenty-seven homers, ninety-nine RBI, and a record twenty-one-for-twenty-one stolen-base mark—split the vote and may have cost Darryl Strawberry the MVP (Dodger Kirk Gibson won). A solid defensive left fielder, the laconic Arkansan may have been too laid back for New York, but he certainly could play. He ended his career as a Mets reserve in 1994.

35. Bobby Ojeda, LHP (1986–1990)

Plucked from the Red Sox, Ojeda was the crafty veteran the pitching staff needed in 1986. The southpaw came through that October after the Mets began both the NLCS and World Series with losses. Bobby O. also started epic Game 6 in both series, and the Mets won both games in dramatic fashion in extra innings. He led the 108-win Mets with eighteen victories and his .783 winning percentage was the NL's best. Injured for much of 1987, Ojeda tossed five shutouts and had a 2.88 ERA the following year; he led the NL with a 4.03 walk-to-strikeout ratio when an accident with hedge clippers abruptly ended his season just as the Mets clinched the 1988 NL East title. He won thirteen games in 1989, but he spent much of 1990—his last year as a Met—in the bullpen. He has since spent plenty of time analyzing the Mets on SNY.

Bobby O.'s Top Five

1. Tom Seaver
2. Dwight Gooden
3. Gary Carter
4. Keith Hernandez
5. Mike Piazza

36. Bobby Jones, RHP (1994–2000)

Jones was selected with a 1991 compensatory pick from the Dodgers, who'd signed Darryl Strawberry. Jones used pinpoint control to lead the Mets in starts and wins twice during his seven seasons with the club; he is among the team's top ten in those categories, along with innings (1,215.2) and strikeouts (714). An All-Star in 1997, his most memorable year as a Met was his last. He went to the minors at the club's request in April 2000 and went 8–2 in the second half with a 3.98 ERA. His one-hit shutout in that year's NLDS clincher was among the best-pitched games in franchise history and brought to mind another Mets right-hander from Fresno, California: Tom Seaver.

37. Wayne Garrett, 3B (1969–1976)

Garrett was the best Rule 5 pick in Mets history, yet the team spent much of the 1970s trying to replace him at third base, trading away Amos Otis and Nolan Ryan in the process. "Red" wound up playing more games at third (709) than any Met until Howard Johnson finally passed him in 1991. Drafted by the Braves—as was older brother Adrian—Wayne was left unprotected by Atlanta and found himself playing regularly at age twenty-one for the 1969 Mets. Garrett hit the go-ahead home run against the Braves in the 1969 NLCS and homered twice in the 1973 World Series, though he made the last out of Game 7. Versatile and patient, the lefty-swinging Garrett drew at least seventy walks four times as a Met and is still in the top five in that category (482).

38. Craig Swan, RHP (1973–1984)

Craig Swan won an ERA crown and not much else as ace of the post-Seaver Mets. Highly touted out of Arizona State, Swan broke into the rotation in 1976 and took over the top spot when Tom Seaver was traded in June of the following year. His 2.43 ERA claimed the NL crown for the ninety-six-loss Mets in 1978, but his fourteen wins for the ninety-nine-loss Mets of 1979 was downright remarkable and represents the most wins by a Met between 1977 and 1983; his ten complete games and 251.1 innings that year were also tops in that span. Injuries caught up with Swan, and he was released in the midst of the club's turnaround in 1984.

39. Al Jackson, LHP (1962–1965, 1968–1969)

Jackson paid his dues with the original Mets, and the Mets have been paying him for close to five decades: first as a crafty southpaw who threw the club's first shutout and got the first Mets win at Shea Stadium, and later as a coach still in uniform in the organization in 2011. How bad were those early Mets? Jackson endured two twenty-loss seasons and was the club's career loss leader until 1974, but he never led the team in losses in any season. He did, however, lead the Mets in wins—with thirteen, eleven, and eight—from 1963 to 1965 (Jackson was the club's career wins leader until Tom Seaver). He was endowed with heart, chutzpah, and a hell of a left arm; luck was another matter. The Mets reacquired him after he was not used by the Cardinals in the 1967 World Series; the Mets released him a few months shy of the 1969 World Series.

40. Robin Ventura, 3B (1999–2001)

Imported from the White Sox after the 1998 season, his arrival shifted Edgardo Alfonzo to second base and created what *Sports Illustrated* argued might be "The Best Infield Ever." Ventura won the Gold Glove in 1999 and set career highs with 32 home runs, 120 RBI, 38 doubles, 177 hits, .301 average, and .528 slugging. He finished sixth in MVP voting while also providing the team theme with "Mojo Risin'" and the "grand slam that wasn't" that still won Game 5 of the NLCS in the fifteenth inning. That year he also became the first player to hit grand slams in both games of a doubleheader. His other two Mets seasons didn't compare, but Ventura provided protection for Mike Piazza, and he surpassed twenty homers each year as a Met.

41. Todd Hundley, C (1991–1998)

This spot on the list would have belonged to Johan Santana, but like Pedro Martinez before him, one magnificent year as a Met turned into an injury-prone Flushing tenure. Hundley was also injured plenty, but besides setting the team home-run mark in 1996 with 41 (tied ten years later by Carlos Beltran), Hundley was just the fourth Met with multiple 30-homer seasons. Through 2011, the switch-hitting catcher stands seventh with 124 homers as a Met and his 724 games caught is third in team annals.

42. Roger McDowell, RHP (1985–1989)

McDowell gets the nod over fellow number 42 Ron Taylor because of five scoreless innings of relief in nail-biting Game 6 of the 1986 NLCS. He got the win in Game 7 of the World Series, though he left a mess for Jesse Orosco. McDowell saved twenty-two games in 1986, threw a career-high 128 innings, won a club record fourteen times in relief, and became the first Met to pitch in seventy games. He picked up the win in Cincinnati on July 22 when he and Orosco alternated between the mound and the outfield in a surreal fourteen-inning victory. Though a renowned prankster, McDowell knew pitching—as evidenced by a long career as a coach—and he saved sixteen or more games in each of his four full seasons with the Mets as Davey Johnson often alternated closers.

43. Ron Taylor, RHP (1967–1971)

The team leader in saves each year from 1967 to 1970, Taylor was one of the few veterans on the Miracle Mets. Though the 1969 starting staff completed the job fifty-one times, Gil Hodges went to the right-handed reliever to finish forty-four games. The Canadian came through with thirteen saves and a 9–4 mark. He picked up the Mets, and the team reciprocated—New York won all four games in which he blew a save. Taylor saved the first Mets World Series victory, getting the final out in Game 2 in Baltimore. He retired and became a doctor, serving as trainer for his hometown Blue Jays.

44. Dave Magadan, 1B-3B (1986–1992)

The Golden Spikes winner at Alabama as the country's best amateur player in 1983, Magadan arrived in the majors with a ballplayer's pedigree as Lou Piniella's cousin. He had three hits in his first start, which also happened to be the night the Mets clinched the 1986 division title. Yet as a corner infielder without power, Magadan had to force his way into the everyday lineup. He entered a mid-June 1990 series at Wrigley Field hitting .301 and playing sporadically when new manager Bud Harrelson began starting him instead of Mike Marshall. A week later, Magadan was a fixture in the number-two hole and was hitting .383. He wound up third in the batting race at .328. His .292 career Mets average remains in the top ten and his .391 on-base percentage was the highest of any Met until John Olerud arrived at the end of the decade. By then, Magadan had been an original Florida Marlin and landed in five other cities as the professional bat off the bench, eventually turning that knowledge into a career as a batting coach.

45. Ron Swoboda, OF (1965–1970)

Good things seemed to happen around Swoboda, most memorably the backhanded, diving grab by Rocky's usually shaky glove to save Game 4 of the 1969 World Series against Baltimore. His eighth-inning double the next day brought in the go-ahead run that Jerry Koosman made stand up for the title. A few weeks earlier, Swoboda's two home runs beat Steve Carlton in St. Louis despite Lefty's nineteen strikeouts to set a new record. Brought to the majors by Casey Stengel at age twenty in 1965, Swoboda never reached the star level that some predicted, but he seemed to come through when all eyes were on the Mets.

46. Ron Hunt, 2B (1963–1966)

Hunt got on base any way possible and gave new meaning to the term "taking one for the team." Hunt has held the Mets hit-by-pitch record since his rookie year of 1963, the longest-held career Mets offensive record. His forty-one HBP in 459 games as a Met still pales next to the major league record fifty he absorbed in 1971 as an Expo. Hunt could hit as well as be hit. He was the first Mets All-Star starter in 1964 and that year became the first Met to bat .300 in more than five hundred plate appearances.

47. Donn Clendenon, 1B (1969–1971)

Donn Clendenon was the imported muscle that the youthful Mets needed in 1969. The only player acquired via trade that year, Clendenon brought brawn and experience to the pesky, young Mets lineup. Still, Gil Hodges often sat Donn against righties—Clendenon did not play at all in the NLCS against righty-dominant Atlanta. The Baltimore lefties brought out the best in Clendenon in the World Series, and he homered three times, including a Game 5 blast minutes after the "Shoe Polish Incident" put Cleon Jones at first base. Clendenon hit .357 with a 1.509 OPS against the O's to earn World Series MVP. (Al Weis, who hit .455, received the Babe Ruth Award from the New York Baseball Writers.) Clendenon's best year as a Met came in 1970, when he set a then–club record with ninety-seven RBI and batted .288.

WAR! What Is It Good For?

The list below looks at the top-fifty Mets ranked according to Wins Above Replacement compiled as Mets. WAR looks at a player's performance based on how valuable he is compared to the average Triple-A player who might be called up to replace him. One thing to keep in mind when looking at these numbers is that baseball has become more offensively oriented in the half century since the Mets were born. And WAR does not take into account postseason play or rate relief pitchers very high in general. Hitters are listed by plate appearances (PA) and pitchers by innings pitched (IP)—to distinguish hitters/PA from pitchers/IP, the latter include a decimal place whether or not their totals included partial innings. Bold indicates the player did not make the *Best Mets* top fifty. Explanations of the players left off the list are also included.

Table 1.3. All-Time Mets Ranked by WAR

Player	*PA/IP*	*WAR*	Best Mets *Rank*
Seaver, Tom	3045.1	75.8	1
Koosman, Jerry	2544.2	41.8	5
Gooden, Dwight	2169.2	41.2	2
Strawberry, Darryl	4549	37.7	3
Wright, David	4335	32.5	6
Beltran, Carlos	3221	31.9	12
Reyes, Jose	4254	29.2	8
Alfonzo, Edgardo	4449	29.1	11
Matlack, Jon	1448.0	27	20
Fernandez, Sid	1584.2	26.9	19
Hernandez, Keith	3684	26.5	7
Leiter, Al	1360.0	26.3	13
Johnson, Howard	4591	24.7	15
Piazza, Mike	3941	24.6	4
Wilson, Mookie	4307	19.4	9
Cone, David	1209.1	19	17

(*continued*)

Player	PA/IP	WAR	Best Mets Rank
Olerud, John	2018	18.6	30
Stearns, John	3080	18.5	24
Jones, Cleon	4683	17.6	10
McReynolds, Kevin	3218	17	34
Darling, Ron	1620.0	16.5	21
Dykstra, Lenny	1908	16.4	26
Magadan, Dave	2483	15.2	44
Harrelson, Bud	5083	14.8	22
Reed, Rick	888.2	14.8	31
Santana, Johan	**600.0**	**14.4**	
Garrett, Wayne	3361	13.2	37
Grote, Jerry	4335	13	23
Mazzilli, Lee	3496	12.9	27
Swan, Craig	1230.2	12.6	38
McGraw, Tug	792.2	12.4	14
Agee, Tommie	2687	12.4	25
Franco, John	702.2	12.4	29
Orosco, Jesse	595.2	12.2	18
Saberhagen, Bret	**524.1**	**11.5**	
Glavine, Tom	**1005.1**	**11.3**	
Carter, Gary	2448	11.2	16
Gilkey, Bernard	**1567**	**11.1**	
Hundley, Todd	2904	10.9	41
Ventura, Robin	1771	10.7	40
Benitez, Armando	**347.0**	**10.6**	
Milner, John	**2755**	**10.1**	
Jones, Bobby	1215.2	9.7	36
Backman, Wally	2704	9.6	32
Ojeda, Bobby	764	9.6	35
Henderson, Steve	**2029**	**9.6**	
Viola, Frank	**566.1**	**9.6**	
Trachsel, Steve	**956.1**	**9.1**	
Johnson, Lance	**1023**	**8.9**	
Floyd, Cliff	**1884**	**8.9**	

Who Missed WAR and Why

Johan Santana, LHP (2008–2011)

A year ago, I put Santana in my Mets top-fifty list for another publication, but after missing yet more time with injuries, Johan joins Pedro Martinez as great pitchers who put together brilliant first seasons in New York only to follow with three shortened seasons for a team unable to contend without their high-priced ace. Sigh.

Bret Saberhagen, RHP (1992–1995)

It's impressive he racked up such a high WAR total in such a short time. His fourteen wins and just thirteen walks in 1994 remain a remarkable legacy, but that same legacy is stained by spraying bleach at a room full of reporters.

Tom Glavine, LHP (2003–2007)

He won his three-hundredth game as a Met, and a lot of people liked him until that final start that ended the 2007 nightmare, followed by his cavalier comments afterward. By comparison, not making the *Best Mets* top-fifty list shouldn't devastate him.

John Milner, 1B (1972–1977)

Milner was more consistent than teammate Dave Kingman, but Kong's moon shots edged the Hammer off the list. It hurt to leave him out.

Bernard Gilkey (1996–1998)

A one-year wonder who helps the Mets contend might sneak into the top fifty, but 1996 can't be that year, given that the Mets lost ninety-one times and contended only in their dreams. Kudos to Gilkey for the career year, hitting .317, tying Howard Johnson's Mets mark of 117 RBI, amassing a club record 44 doubles, and collecting a lucrative four-year deal.

Bobby Bonilla, 3B-OF (1992–1995)

Bonilla amassed stats for a lifeless team and was brutal at third base and the outfield. He'll still be getting paid $1.19 million in annual deferred payments from the Mets through 2035, so he'll live without making this cut.

Armando Benitez, RHP (1999–2003)

History and histrionics play a part in the list. Armando is second all-time in saves for the Mets, but he is first in torching key ballgames in September and October.

Steve Henderson, OF (1977–1980)

Spending fewer than four seasons in New York—four of the darkest seasons in Mets history, no less—keeps Hendu out of the top fifty. Lord knows, he was the best player of the four that Cincinnati sent east in the cataclysmic Tom Seaver trade. Henderson provided a lot of effort and a few timely hits for a Mets team that lost an average of ninety-seven games per season during his tenure. Thank you for trying, Steve.

Frank Viola, LHP (1989–1991)

Like Bret Saberhagen, Viola had one outstanding year in New York and wasn't all that great otherwise. The homegrown Long Island lefty is the last twenty-game winner in Mets history, reaching the milestone in the last game of 1990.

Steve Trachsel, RHP (2001–2006)

Trachsel had a better WAR than Al Jackson, Ron Taylor, or Roger Mc-Dowell, but I would go to war with any of those guys over a pitcher who basically gave up in the first inning of a playoff game in a tied series in 2006. The glacially slow-working Trachsel would make the top-five most-frustrating Mets pitchers to watch.

Lance Johnson, OF (1996–1997)

It would be preposterous to have a player who played less than two seasons in New York in the top fifty, but "One-Dog" almost pulled it off. If Steve Phillips hadn't swapped him to the Cubs in August of 1997 for Brian McRae (also bringing back Turk Wendell), Johnson might still be landing hits in Flushing. His 227 hits, 21 triples, and 75 multi-hit games in 1996 have already lasted fifteen years and withstood assaults from Jose Reyes in his prime.

Cliff Floyd, OF (2003–2006)

If this was a list of the fifty coolest Mets, then Cliff would be in the top ten. He ambled to the plate with the theme to *Sanford and Son* on the P.A. and gave it everything he had, both in the field and at the plate. And he sure could speak his mind. Unfortunately, Floyd was also frequently injured, putting together just one season of more than 107 starts in left field.

Made Cut for *Best Mets* List but Not According to WAR

Player	PA/IP	WAR	Best Mets Rank
Hunt, Ron	1887	7.8	46
Staub, Rusty	2965	7.6	28
Millan, Felix	2954	6.2	49
Swoboda, Ron	2485	5.9	45
Taylor, Ron	361	4.8	43
McDowell, Roger	468.1	4.7	42
Jackson, Al	980.2	4.5	39
Kranepool, Ed	5997	4.4	33
Kingman, Dave	2573	3.2	50
Clendenon, Donn	957	3.1	47
Knight, Ray	932	2.1	48

Note: All stats are through 2011 season. PA is plate appearances; IP is innings pitched; and WAR is Wins Above Replacement.

The Fans' Top Five

1. Tom Seaver
2. Mike Piazza
3. Dwight Gooden
4. Darryl Strawberry
5. Jose Reyes

This is from a survey conducted by *USA Today Sports Weekly* in June 2011; 81 percent of the more-than-twenty-seven-hundred voters pulled the lever for Seaver.

48. Ray Knight, 3B (1984–1986)

Though he spent just two years and one month as a Met, Knight's 1986 World Series MVP earns his place on this list. In the NLCS, he tied Game 6 in the ninth inning and put the Mets ahead for good seven innings later. In Game 6 of the World Series, his two-out single kept the miraculous rally alive, and he danced home with the winning run on Bill Buckner's error. His Game 7 homer snapped a tie in the seventh inning. Knight hit .391 with a 1.005 OPS in what was his last action as a Met. Known for his marriage to golfing great Nancy Lopez and for being in the middle of Mets fisticuffs, Knight's .298 average in 1986 was an improvement of eighty points over the previous year.

49. Felix Millan, 2B (1973–1977)

"Felix the Cat" choked up on the bat as much as anyone since the Deadball era and was impossible to strike out. Second to Wally Backman with 654 games at second base as a Met, Millan was the only man in the club's first fifty years to start all 162 games in a season. That same year, 1975, he set the club marks for hits (191) and doubles (37), both since surpassed. Millan's Mets career ended abruptly when he was slammed to the turf during a 1977 fight in Pittsburgh.

50. Dave Kingman, 1B-OF (1975–1977, 1981–1983)

Kingman was voted the National League's All-Star right fielder in 1976 and had a realistic shot at Hack Wilson's NL mark of fifty-six home runs

... until he injured his thumb diving for a ball in late July. He lost almost a month and, stuck on thirty-two home runs, lost the NL home-run lead by one to Mike Schmidt, 38–37. Though sent to San Diego in the 1977 "Midnight Massacre," Kong returned to Shea in 1981 and became the first Met to claim a home-run crown with thirty-seven in 1982. Kingman didn't make contact (a strikeout every 3.4 at bats as a Met), hit for average (.219 Mets mark), draw walks (.287 OBP), or field (thirty-one errors in 199 games at first base in 1981–1982). But fans loved Kong, the first Met with multiple thirty-homer seasons and bringer of the tape-measure shot to Shea.

Mets People

Jane Jarvis: "The Queen of Melody"

Enter Shea Stadium on any day during the Ed Kranepool Flushing Era (1964–1979), and the air was filled with a melodious—never overpowering—sound of organ music. Despite contrary harmonic assurances, Mets fans of the 1960s and 1970s were not guaranteed to have the time of their life every time they stepped into Shea, but they would be guaranteed to hear the music of Jane Jarvis.

Born Luella Jane Nossett, the only child of a lawyer and a schoolteacher, the thirteen-year-old maestro was playing jazz for friends in her Indiana home in 1929 when a telephone call informed her that her parents had been killed in an accident. An only child, Jarvis made her own way as a musician, studying at the Chicago Conservatory of Music. The first baseball game she ever attended was a paying gig. The Braves asked Jarvis, then host of her own show, *Jivin' With Jarvis*, to be organist at Milwaukee County Stadium in 1954. Though she was reluctant at first, she took the job and embraced the game, providing background music for eight years of Braves baseball—including two World Series. After she moved to New York, the Braves asked if she'd be interested in joining them after they moved to Atlanta. She said no, but asked for an introduction to George Weiss of the Mets.

The Mets hired Jarvis in 1964. She mixed in jazz favorites, "Scrapple from the Apple," contemporary standards, "Cabaret," and ballpark standards, "Take Me Out to the Ballgame." Her version of "Meet the Mets" was far jazzier than the recorded version that all Mets fans knew. Walking up to Shea on sunny afternoons and hearing her organ made it almost feel like the orange-and-blue panels were floating musical notes circling the big, round stadium. Many a child—and grownup—begged to stay through the seventh-inning stretch to hear her incomparable version of "The Mexican Hat Dance."

Perhaps her greatest service to both fans and the city occurred on July 13, 1977. During a stifling Tuesday night game against the Cubs, the lights went out in the sixth inning. The blackout was a nightmare in many parts of New York, with wholesale looting and nearly four thousand people arrested, but Jarvis restored calm and a "hey, we came here to go to a ballgame" feeling to the crowd of ten thousand. She played Christmas songs that everyone could sing along with. Jarvis provided dignity in what was one of the team's worst seasons in her tenure. Although she played accompanying music to two Shea Stadium World Series, the Mets had losing records in nine of her seasons there.

"They had no substitute for me, and they never got one. They've been using records ever since."

Jarvis had a day job at Muzak corporation, starting as a secretary and rising to vice president. Whereas most musicians always look for a larger audience, Jarvis sought a smaller one. She left Muzak and the Mets in successive years and, at age sixty-four, looked to go on her own again as a jazz pianist. "I realized that no one would ever take me seriously in jazz if I stayed with the Mets," she told the *New York Times* in 1984. "They had no substitute for me, and they never got one. They've been using records ever since." It's never been the same.

She returned to Shea as a guest during its final season in 2008 and died at age ninety-four in 2010. To those who recall—or can at least appreciate—the days when the outside of the stadium was orange and blue and the inside was free of blaring pumped-in noise, Jane Jarvis lives on.

Best Mets Teams

⚾ Top-Five Teams Profile ⚾

1. The 1969 Mets

Why So High? Who could argue with the Shea Stadium scoreboard the night of September 10, 1969, when the Mets took over first place for the first time in franchise history? "Look Who's Number One," the big board read. The Mets made up ten games in the standings in just twenty-seven days. And the next month was even more Amazin'.

Ranked Ahead of: 1986 Mets. The only other world champion Mets team was the lone challenger for the top spot, but at the end of the day, you never forget your first. The franchise, birthed into being as a 120-loss catastrophe in 1962, headed into 1969 as a 100-1 underdog in Las Vegas to win the World Series. Place your retroactive bets!

Mets Valuable Player: Tom Seaver and **Jerry Koosman.** Yes, sharing this honor sounds like a cop-out, but the Mets wouldn't have gotten to the World Series without Seaver, and they wouldn't have won the Series without Koosman. Tom was Terrific, with an "Imperfect Game" thrown in, going 25–7 with a 2.21 ERA while winning the Cy Young Award and Sportsman of the Year from *Sports Illustrated*. In just his second season in the majors, Kooz went 17–9 with a 2.28 ERA and rebounded from a dreadful start in Atlanta in the NLCS to dominate in his World Series appearances. He took a no-hitter into the seventh inning of Game 2 in Baltimore and won, 2–1. After Seaver won Game 4 in ten innings, Kooz allowed just one hit and one walk after the third inning of Game 5 and got Davey Johnson to fly out in the ninth to send New York into uninhibited delirium.

Other Great Performances: Cleon Jones's .340 average remained the club record for twenty-nine years and his shoe polish helped fuel a rally in the decisive game against the Orioles; Cleon's high school classmate, Tommie Agee, hit the only home run into Shea's upper deck and led the team in homers (26) and RBI (76) from the leadoff spot—he also made two of the most incredible catches in World Series history . . . in the same game; relievers Ron Taylor and Tug McGraw gave the Mets a two-headed, two-armed bullpen stopper with McGraw going twelve-for-twelve in save chances and both relievers winning nine times; World Series MVP Donn Clendenon came over from Montreal to provide a much needed power bat; and don't forget light-hitting second baseman Al Weis, who also filled in for a month at shortstop, providing crucial late-game hits in both Koosman World Series starts to earn the Babe Ruth Award for the World Series.

This Magic Moment: There are so many to choose from: Seaver's "Imperfect Game" in July stamped the Mets as contenders; the twin double-header sweeps of San Diego despite scoring just ten runs in four games that began the road to the title in mid-August; the incredible play started by Rod Gaspar in extra innings that saved the game in a Mets win in San Francisco; "The Black Cat" on the field in September proved a good omen for the Mets and fatal for the Cubs; and there was Ron Swoboda, who'd homered twice to beat Steve Carlton in his record nineteen-strikeout game in St. Louis and made a stupendous diving catch to save Game 4 against the Orioles. The one moment that says it all about the Miracle Mets, however, was the "Shoe Polish Incident." Down 3–0 in the sixth inning of Game 5 of the World Series, a pitch bounced near Cleon Jones's foot, and Gil Hodges emerged from the dugout with a ball with shoe polish on it (whose shoe polish it was remains a question). Jones was sent to first and Donn Clendenon followed with a home run. Al Weis homered an inning later, Swoboda knocked in the lead run in the eighth, and Koosman set down the O's in the ninth for as unlikely a world championship as baseball has ever seen.

You Might Forget That . . . Despite the clutch hits that produced eleven walkoff wins and forty-three one-run victories, the 1969 Mets were not a great-hitting team. This championship was a true team effort and was achieved with an offense that finished eighth in hitting (.242), ninth in scoring (3.90 per game), and eleventh in on-base plus slugging (.662) . . . and keep in mind in 1969 there were two first-year expansion clubs that lost 110 times each to beat up on. The Mets had been first-year patsies themselves just seven years earlier. They knew what to do now.

Record Setters: The pitching staff carried the 1969 Mets, pure and simple. While 1969 was just one season removed from the "Year of the Pitcher," the lowered mound and smaller strike zone helped reintroduce offense to baseball; the 1969 Mets pitching staff did everything possible to kill it. The Mets had a 2.99 ERA and a league-best twenty-eight shutouts and 1.181 walks and hits per inning. A staff with an average age of 25.8 years, and pitching in a pennant race for the first time, embarked on a thirty-six-inning shutout streak in mid-September. It included a doubleheader sweep in Pittsburgh in which the Mets won both games 1–0, with the pitcher driving in the only run in each. In late September, they put together forty-two straight shutout innings that included Gary Gentry blanking the Cards for the NL East title and a weekend in Philadelphia without a run crossing home plate. Ten innings in those streaks belonged to 1969 Met Nolan Ryan—the staff was so good that the young, wild Ryan mostly sat.

Attendance: 2,175,373—highest to that point at Shea Stadium.

Indelible Image: Jerry Koosman leaping into Jerry Grote's arms and Ed Charles dancing on the mound moments after the Miracle landed and moments before all hell broke loose on the field.

1969 Baseball Roundup

NLCS: Mets sweep NL West champ Braves, 3–0.
ALCS: Orioles sweep AL West champ Twins, 3–0.

World Series: Mets defeat Orioles, 4–1.

NL MVP: Willie McCovey, Giants.

NL Cy Young: Tom Seaver, Mets.

NL Rookie of the Year: Ted Sizemore, Dodgers.

Hall of Fame Inductees: Stan Musial, Roy Campanella, Waite Hoyt, Stan Covelski.

Elsewhere

Top News Stories: Vietnam, the moon landing, Chappaquiddick, Woodstock.

Top Sports Stories: The Jets—a Shea tenant—upset the Colts in Super Bowl III preceding the Mets' championship; the Knicks won the NBA title for 1969–1970.

Best Picture Winner: *Midnight Cowboy.*

Top-Selling U.S. Album: *In-A-Gadda-Da-Vida,* by Iron Butterfly.

Price of Bread: 20 cents.

Price of a Box Seat at Shea Stadium: $3.50.

2. The 1986 Mets

Why Not Number One? As incredible as pulling out the 1986 NLCS and World Series were, the Mets were the favored team. The writers laughed at Gil Hodges when he said the 1969 Mets would be above .500. It's a close call, but 1969 gets the nod. If it's dominating Mets ball clubs you're looking for, however, you may never see a team that decimated opponents in the regular season like this Mets team.

Ranked Ahead of: 1973 Mets. The last Mets team prior to 1986 to win the NL East title, the 1973 Mets almost pulled off another miraculous upset. The Mets finished fifth or lower and with a losing record eight times between 1974 and 1983. Yet the mid-1980s Mets had the only pitching staff that can be mentioned in the same breath as the bumper-arms crop the franchise produced from 1968 to 1977. The 1986 Mets had six pitchers win in double digits, and their lead did not shrink from double digits after June 30. The final 1986 margin in the NL East was 21½ games.

Mets Valuable Player: Bobby Ojeda. He was the main difference in the team between 1985 and 1986. The twenty-eight-year-old Bobby O. was the elder statesman in the rotation and carried an intensity you can still grab a piece of watching his dispatches on SNY. His 2.57 ERA over 217 innings was second to Houston's Mike Scott—Ojeda was likewise second in adjusted ERA—and Bobby O. was third with a 1.091 WHIP. Churning out an 18–5 mark with seven complete games, Ojeda was simply a better pitcher in the National League than he'd been before the December 1985 trade with Boston—and he was no doubt helpful with information about his former team come World Series time. After the Mets started both postseason series with losses, Ojeda got the team off the schneid with superb performances, and though he didn't get the win in either epic Game 6 that October, he certainly kept his club close.

Other Great Performances: It truly was a team effort. How about the rotation takes a bow? The first four pitchers among the winning percentage leaders were all Mets: Bobby Ojeda (.783), Dwight Gooden (.739), Sid Fernandez (.727), and Ron Darling (.714). They also had three in the top five in ERA: Ojeda (2.57), Darling (2.81), and Gooden (2.84). Rick Aguilera also won ten, while Roger McDowell set a club record with seventy-five appearances and fourteen wins out of the pen. McDowell and Jesse Orosco had twenty saves each, and they both got the job done as needed in the postseason, winning or saving seven of the eight October triumphs. WAR-wise (Wins Above Replacement), Keith Hernandez (5.6) and Lenny Dykstra (4.9) led the club. Gary Carter and Hernandez finished third and fourth, respectively, in the MVP voting; their combined home run total (37) equaled that of Mike Schmidt, who won the award for the third time. Cy Young winner Mike Scott of Houston also got the NLCS MVP, though Lenny Dykstra and Orosco had strong cases. The Mets were content with the World Series trophy.

This Magic Moment: The one that burns brightest a quarter century later is Game 6. Down by two runs with two outs in the tenth inning, it sure looked over. Then Gary Carter singled, Kevin Mitchell singled, and Ray Knight's hit brought in a run and put men on the corners. Bob Stanley came in, and Mookie Wilson jackknifed away from the wild pitch that plated the tying run. Then there was a ground ball to Bill Buckner . . . but let's not overshadow Game 7 and the sixth-inning rally from 3–0 down off Bruce Hurst, who'd beaten the Mets twice. Sid Fernandez's stellar relief kept the Mets in the game, Keith Hernandez's two-run single made it a game, and Carter's RBI tied the game. Ray Knight's homer snapped the tie, and the Mets tacked on runs that made that night quite magical as well. And three wins in their last at bat in the NLCS ain't chopped liver.

You Might Forget That . . . The Mets were supposed to have home-field advantage in the NLCS, but a Bears-Oilers NFL game was scheduled on Sunday at the Astrodome, so the Mets lost a home game. Fortunately, the Mets didn't have to test fate or Mike Scott's scuffball with a game 7 in Houston. And Jesse Orosco, who got the last out for both the pennant and World Series came to the Mets from the Twins for Jerry Koosman, who had thrown the final pitch when the Mets clinched the 1969 world championship.

Record Setters: The 108 wins (and 54 losses) are records that will be hard to surpass. The team batted a then–club record .263, leading the National League in that category as well as runs (783), hits (1,462), on-base percentage (.339), slugging (.401), and OPS (.740). It marked the first time the Mets had led the NL in any of these categories in their twenty-five seasons of existence. Individually, the Mets had such a big lead that players were regularly rested, so no significant individual records were set—except when it came to making money. George Foster, making the most money of any player in major league history at $2.8 million in 1986, was released by the Mets in August. (Postseason hero Gary Carter was second in the majors in salary at $2.16 million.)

Attendance: 2,762,417—the highest to that point at Shea Stadium. (Their road attendance of 2,180,166 was likewise the highest to that point in team history.)

Indelible Image: Jesse Orosco's glove goes flying after Game 7 at Shea in the World Series. Orosco's NLCS clinching celebration was similarly joyous— and the plane ride from Houston to New York channeled Keith Moon when it came to destroying private property.

1986 Baseball Roundup

NLCS: Mets defeat NL West champ Astros, 4–2.
ALCS: Red Sox defeat AL West champ Angels, 4–3.
World Series: Mets defeat Red Sox, 4–3.
NL MVP: Mike Schmidt, Phillies.
NL Cy Young: Mike Scott, Astros.
NL Rookie of the Year: Todd Worrell, Cardinals.
Hall of Fame Inductees: Willie McCovey, Bobby Doerr, Ernie Lombardi.

Elsewhere

Top News Stories: United States bombs Gaddafi in Libya; Chernobyl and Perestroika are two separate stunning events in USSR.
Top Sports Stories: The Giants win their first Super Bowl, defeating the Broncos, whose epic drive in the AFC Championship Game had broken Cleveland's heart.
Best Picture Winner: *Platoon.*
Top-Selling U.S. Album: *Whitney Houston.*
Price of Gas: 89 cents (gallon).
Price of a Box Seat at Shea Stadium: $9.50.

3. The 1973 Mets

Why They're Ranked Where They Are: Even more so than 1969, the 1973 Mets were a lightning bolt thrown from the sky. The 1973 Mets played like a last place team for five months, but with one month of great play, they stole a division, a pennant, and came within one game of grand theft championship.

Ranked Ahead of: 1999 Mets. Whereas the 1999 club had strategist showman Bobby Valentine at the helm, the 1973 Mets had word jumbler Yogi Berra, who had been part of sixteen World Series as a player, manager, and coach. What was one more? The 1973 Mets also had two Hall of Famers on the roster: Tom Seaver, in his prime, and Willie Mays, breaking down at the end of a career that had started so long ago. The 1973 and 1999 Mets are the only teams in franchise history to qualify for the postseason by winning their final game of the regular season. Here's to more of that.

Mets Valuable Player: Tug McGraw. Yes, Tom Seaver won the Cy Young, not to mention the division- and pennant-clinching games, but McGraw fueled the big push with his screwball (batters hit .184 off him in the final two months) and his slogan ("Ya gotta believe" got the city behind the team, though the stands weren't crowded until the final home stand). Seaver started seven times in the final month, going 4–2 with a 3.94 ERA in forty-eight innings, shoulder fatigue making him more hittable than he'd been all year. McGraw, who'd been brutal and as responsible as anyone for sinking the Mets 12½ games back in July, completely turned it around. He pitched fifteen times out of the pen during their thirty-eight-game run to the top, winning four, saving ten, and compiling an 0.88 ERA over his final forty-one innings. To cap off the perfect month, McGraw's wife Phyllis gave birth to a son, Mark. (Another son, Tim, who would go on to his own fame in country music, had been born to another mother in 1967.)

"Ya gotta believe!"—reliever Tug McGraw

Other Great Performances: Seaver went 19–10 with a 2.08 ERA covering 290 innings, with a league-best 251 strikeouts and eighteen complete games. Jerry Koosman and Jon Matlack both finished with losing records due to poor support, but they came through big as the Mets made their run. Matlack, whose skull was fractured by a line drive in May, tossed a one-hitter a couple of weeks later and fanned 205 for the year, and he had nine more K's in a two-hit shutout that evened the NLCS in Game 2. Matlack started three times in the World Series, though he lost Game 7. Nine of Koosman's last ten starts were won by the Mets, including the game that clinched at least a tie for the division title. The Mets won all three of Kooz's postseason starts as well. George Stone had a career year at 12–3 with a 2.80 ERA. Long after the Mets lost the World Series, revisionists insisted that Stone—rather than Seaver on short rest—should have started Game 6, with the Mets just needing to win one of the last two games in Oakland. That is all Stone is remembered for today, but people should recall that the deal that brought him from Atlanta to New York—with second baseman Felix Millan—was probably the best trade the Mets made in the 1970s. Rusty Staub, acquired a year earlier from Montreal, led the club with seventy-six RBI and a .781 OPS.

This Magic Moment: A funky carom was the defining play for this club. Four games into a five-game showdown with first-place Pittsburgh, the Mets were down to their last out at Shea when pinch hitter Duffy Dyer doubled home the tying run. Four innings later, a Dave Augustine drive seemed destined for the visitor's bullpen. The ball hit the top of the wall, but instead of bouncing off the ledge and into the pen for a home run—as physics would seem to command—the ball caromed the other way, right to left fielder Cleon Jones. He threw the ball to Wayne Garrett, who gunned it to Ron Hodges, who tagged out Richie Zisk to end the top of the thirteenth. Hodges ended the game in the bottom of the inning with an RBI single. The Mets took over first place the next night, reaching the .500 mark for the first time since May.

"It ain't over til it's over."—*Yogi Berra*

You Might Forget That . . . After the fabled scuffle in Game 3 of the NLCS between Pete Rose and Bud Harrelson that resulted in several Mets having to go to left field to beg fans not to throw debris at Rose, Charlie Hustle exacted some revenge the next day. As banners flew proclaiming "Rose Is a Weed," which was among the kinder sentiments at Shea, Rose homered off Harry Parker in the twelfth inning, rounding the bases with a fist raised. The best-of-five series ended the following day, however, with the Mets beating Cincinnati. Rose ran off the field dodging marauding fans like Bills running back O .J. Simpson would two months later at Shea, when he became the first player to rush for two thousand yards.

Record Setters: No team in major league history had ever qualified for the postseason with such a puny winning percentage as .509. The 1973 Mets mark of 82–79 was finally eclipsed thirty-two years later—with the number of postseason entrants doubled—when the Padres went 82–80 (.506) to finish atop the truly lousy 2005 NL West . . . by five games!

As the Mets made their run in September 1973, Jerry Koosman set a still-standing Mets record with 31.2 consecutive shutout innings. The 1973 Mets may have risen through the standings fast, but their speed on the bases was glacial. The Mets stole just twenty-seven bases all year, the lowest output in club history over a full season. (The 1994 Mets stole just twenty-five, but the last forty-nine games of the year were wiped out by a strike.)

Attendance: 1,722,209—Shea's lowest since 1967.

Indelible Image: The bullpens and dugouts emptying for the wild brawl that ensued after Pete Rose flattened Bud Harrelson in the NLCS, but it was more of a lasting sound than an image—Rose would be booed lustily by the Shea Stadium crowd for the rest of his long career. The World Series provided a memorable image during the tenth inning of Game 2: when Bud Harrelson was called out at home on a phantom tag by A's catcher Ray Fosse, Willie Mays was on his knees begging umpire Augie Donatelli, who, like Mays, would never be at home plate in a major league game after that Series.

1973 Baseball Roundup

NLCS: Mets defeat NL West champ Reds, 3–2.
ALCS: A's defeat AL East champ Orioles, 3–2.
World Series: A's defeat Mets, 4–3.
NL MVP: Pete Rose, Reds (Boo!).
NL Cy Young: Tom Seaver, Mets.
NL Rookie of the Year: Gary Matthews, Giants.
Hall of Fame Inductees: Roberto Clemente, Warren Spahn, Monte Irvin, Mickey Welch, Highpockets Kelly, Billy Evans.

Elsewhere

Top News Stories: U.S. troops withdraw from Vietnam, Watergate hearings, oil embargo, stock market crash.
Top Sports Stories: Knicks become the first team to beat two sixty-win teams (Celtics and Lakers) to claim NBA title; Dolphins complete undefeated season in Super Bowl VII; Secretariat wins horse racing's Triple Crown.
Best Picture Winner: *The Sting.*
Top-Selling U.S. Album: *The World Is a Ghetto* by War.
Price of Gas: 40 cents (gallon).
Price of a Box Seat at Shea Stadium: $3.50.

Table 2.1.   First-Place Mets Teams

Year	Record	Pct.	GA	Manager
1969[a]	100–62	.617	+8	Hodges
1973[b]	92–79	.509	+1½	Berra
1986[a]	108–54	.667	+21½	Johnson
1988[c]	100–60	.625	+15	Johnson
2006[c]	97–65	.599	+12	Randolph

[a] World champions

[b] Won pennant

[c] Lost in NLCS

Note: The Mets also reached the postseason in 1999 and 2000 as Wild-Card winners, finishing second both times. They reached the NLCS in 1999 and took the pennant in 2000.

4. The 1999 Mets

Why They're Ranked Where They Are: This is the most exciting Mets team that did not reach the World Series. They had no-name ballplayers performing at a high level in pressure games—Benny Agbayani, Melvin Mora, Pat Mahomes, and of course, Todd Pratt—but they also had All-Star–caliber players like Mike Piazza, John Olerud, Edgardo Alfonzo, and Al Leiter. And they had a defiant manager (Bobby Valentine) who took on writers, players, and the general manager, and could impersonate Groucho Marx. As Amazin' a year as Shea had seen in quite a while.

Ranked Ahead of: The 2000 Mets. The 1999 Mets had to confront their nemesis Braves head on, while the 2000 Mets caught a huge break when the Cardinals stunned Atlanta in the Division Series. True, once the Mets dispatched the Cards in the NLCS, they had an even more grating archenemy in the Yankees waiting, but the three successive weekends of triumph at Shea in 1999 was a page out of 1969. Amazin'. But the Kenny Rogers walkoff walk to end the 1999 NLCS sure was Aggravatin'.

Mets Valuable Player: Mike Piazza. He justified that seven-year contract soon enough. He amassed 40 homers and 124 RBI, while producing a .303/.361/.575 line scoring 100 runs and starting 136 times behind the plate. It stands as a tribute to the depth of this team that when Piazza injured his thumb in the Division Series, backup Todd Pratt stepped in and became a Mets hero for the ages.

Other Great Performances: The team was built around Piazza, but the Mets have rarely had such pieces to build with: John Olerud (125 walks, 107 runs, 19 HR, 96 RBI, .298/.427/.463), Edgardo Alfonzo (then club-record 123 runs, 27 HR, 108 RBI, .304/.385/.502), Robin Ventura (32 HR, 120 RBI, .301/.379/.529), Rickey Henderson (37 steals, 89 runs, 30 doubles, .315/.423/.466), and Roger Cedeno, yes, Roger Cedeno (then–club-record 66 steals, 90 runs, .313/.396/.408). Beyond this wholly unMetslike offense, they had the best infield in franchise history and made *Sports Illustrated* wonder aloud on its cover whether it was "The Best Infield Ever." Plus rookie Benny Agbayani slammed ten home runs in his first seventy-three at bats. A finger injury to John Franco allowed Armando Benitez to step in as closer and accrue twenty-two saves (Franco had nineteen). The pen was solid yet no starter surpassed the thirteen wins by forty-year-old Orel Hershiser or had an ERA below 4.00. Al Leiter had a so-so year but had the game of his life in the one-game playoff in Cincinnati, while Kenny Rogers was solid at 5–1 with two complete games—though his exit as a Met was far from stellar.

"Mr. Mojo Risin'" —Jim Morrison, reinterpreted by Robin Ventura

---

This Magic Moment: The moments flowed wild, wet, and happy over the first three weekends of October at Shea. The first saw the Mets rise from the dead and gain a tie for the Wild Card when Melvin Mora touched home plate on a walkoff wild pitch in the final regular-season game. After the Mets beat the Reds in the one-game playoff and took a two-games-to-one lead in the Division Series against Arizona, understudy Todd Pratt's home run set Shea shaking and put the Mets in the Championship Series. Once there, the Mets fell behind three games to none and trailed late against Atlanta in Games 4 and 5 before scoring twice in their last at bat to win each time. The greatest of these moments was Robin Ventura, he of the rallying cry from the Doors 1971 album *L.A. Woman,* being stopped at first base for celebratory hugs to create the "Grand Slam Single."

"Get your ass back in the clubhouse where you've been the past two weeks!"—Bobby Valentine to Bobby Bonilla after the latter refused to pinch-hit

You Might Forget That . . . A seven-game losing streak after Memorial Day had General Manager Steve Phillips firing three of Valentine's coaches. The relationship between manager and GM was never the same after that, and neither were the Mets. New York embarked on a 64–30 run that lasted through the summer and ended in late September as the Mets headed to Atlanta trailing by one game in the NL East. Extricating his team from the slide that followed, which coincided with an unfavorable *Sports Illustrated* piece, was perhaps Bobby V.'s greatest trick in New York.

Record Setters: The team's .279 batting average in 1999 remains the highest in club history, along with the club's 853 runs, 814 RBI, and 717 walks.

The 617 walks by the pitching staff, however, were the most in club history, and the 691 earned runs allowed were the most since the laughingstock 1962 Mets, but that's where the magnificent infield came in handy. The Mets allowed just twenty unearned runs all season and committed only sixty-eight errors, both stats shattering major league marks.

Edgardo Alfonzo had a night to remember in Houston on August 30. He became the first Met with six hits in a game, while also setting club records with six runs and sixteen total bases and tying the franchise mark with three homers in a 17–1 demolition of the Astros.

Attendance: 2,725,920—including three sellouts against the Yankees, the first time both teams hosted interleague home games against each other in the same season.

Indelible Image: Bobby Valentine detractors would say the lasting image of 1999 is the manager donned in sunglasses and an eye-black mustache after sneaking into the dugout following an ejection (he was suspended for two games). But the image that will live on is Robin Ventura being lifted in the air after clearing the fence with the bases full to beat the Braves in the fifteenth inning of a rain-soaked NLCS epic. When Todd Pratt, the runner on first, embraced Ventura in the base path, the home run was voided for passing the runner. The go-ahead run still crossed the plate and the final score was 4–3 instead of 7–3. The Mets' last-inning luck ran out in Game 6, but that's an image best left undeveloped.

1999 Baseball Roundup

NLDS: Mets defeat NL West champ Diamondbacks, 3–1.
NLCS: NL East champ Braves defeat Mets, 4–2.
World Series: Yankees defeat Braves, 4–0.
NL MVP: Chipper Jones, Braves.
NL Cy Young: Randy Johnson, Diamondbacks.
NL Rookie of the Year: Scott Williamson, Reds.
Hall of Fame Inductees: George Brett, Nolan Ryan, Robin Yount, Orlando Cepeda, Nestor Chylak, Frank Selee, Smokey Joe Williams.

Elsewhere

Top News Stories: Columbine shootings; Euro currency introduced in eleven countries.
Top Sports Stories: United States wins first Women's World Cup on penalty kicks; Lance Armstrong wins his first Tour de France.
Best Picture Winner: *American Beauty.*
Top-Selling U.S. Album: *Millennium* by Backstreet Boys.
Price of Gas: $1.22 (gallon).
Price of a Box Seat at Shea Stadium: $25.

5. The 2000 Mets

Why They're Ranked Where They Are: The 2000 Mets got to the World Series, while their 1999 predecessors did not, but walking in the winning run in extra innings in the NLCS is still preferable to losing at home to the Yankees in the World Series. If you weren't old enough to experience these years, trust me on this.

Ranked Ahead of: 2006 Mets. The 2000 Mets got to the World Series. The 2006 NLCS loss to the Cardinals was even more gut-wrenching than the way 2000 ended and even worse than 1988 (though the 1988 and 2006 seven-game losses are eerily similar).

Mets Valuable Player: Well, since we made Mike Piazza team MVP for 1999, it seems only fair for **Edgardo Alfonzo** to represent 2000. Many of Alfonzo's counting stats were lower than the previous year because he played slightly less and wound up with seventy-six fewer plate appearances. He still clubbed 25 home runs, scored 109, and drove in 94, while increasing his walk total by 10 and cutting down his strikeouts by 15. His .324/.425/.542 line was the best of his career, his Wins Above Replacement (6.7) was a full point higher, and his OPS plus was 22 points ahead of 1999. He drove in five in the NLDS, including the game-tying double in the eighth inning of Game 3, and he batted .444 against the Cardinals in the NLCS. He made the All-Star team for the only time in his career. Always under the radar, but always coming through—the Fonz didn't need hype to be cool.

Other Great Performances: Mike Piazza had perhaps his best season as a Met. Todd Zeile was no John Olerud with bat or glove, but he had a solid first season as a first baseman in New York, with twenty-two home runs and ten errors. Benny Agbayani, who was supposed to go down to the minors in April, stayed with the team all year and had a 122 OPS plus. The entire rotation won in double figures, including new members Mike Hampton and Glendon Rusch. All-Star Al Leiter fanned two hundred and was brilliant throughout the season all the way until his last pitch in the World Series. Reinvented as setup men, John Franco and Turk Wendell made the seventh and eighth innings easier for the Mets and cleared the way for Armando Benitez.

"The Mets have never had a better game pitched in their 39-year history than this game pitched by Bobby Jones." —Bob Murphy, NLDS clincher

---

This Magic Moment: The home run by Mike Piazza to cap a ten-run inning after the Mets were down 8–1 in the eighth inning on Fireworks Night was special. The twenty-four hours of Shea-hem—triggered by Benny Agbayani's thirteenth-inning home run followed the next day by the Bobby Jones one-hit clincher in the NLDS—was tremendous. But the bases-clearing triple by Todd Zeile in Game 5 of the NLCS that put the Mets up 6–0 and punched their ticket to their first World Series since 1986 had Shea swaying in euphoria like few moments in the life of that big old ballpark. The Mets won the pennant while 1999 Mets John Olerud and Rickey Henderson, members of the 2000 Mariners, were still battling the Yankees in the ALCS. We could dream of different outcomes, no?

"It was a reckless type of action on his part. . . . I don't think Roger Clemens intended the barrel of the bat to hit Mike Piazza." —MLB discipline czar Frank Robinson

---

You Might Forget That . . . The 2000 Mets had the franchise's patented September swoon, like the 1998 and 1999 clubs—and let's not even start about the nightmares to come in 2007 and 2008. The 2000 Mets, however, weathered the storm in the first week of September instead of the last. The Mets entered Labor Day weekend with the best record in the National League and held a half-game lead on Atlanta, but three straight walkoff losses in St. Louis kicked off a 1–7 stretch that saw the Mets drop into the Wild-Card spot, which they retained with little drama with a 14–6 finish. The final standings show the Mets finishing one game behind the Braves at 94–68, but that was the result of winning their last five after the Braves clinched the NL East at Shea during the final week. The Mets were eight games better than Davey Johnson's Dodgers in the Wild-Card standings.

Record Setters: The Mets set a franchise record by belting 198 home runs (the 2006 Mets hit a couple more). Four 2000 Mets clubbed at least 20 home runs; and seven finished in double digits. "Monster Out of the Cage" Mike Piazza hit 38 homers and established club records over a full season for slugging (.614) and OPS (1.012).

Speaking of homers, Mike Bordick and Bubba Trammell both went deep the first time they batted as Mets following deadline trades. Trammell came in a savvy deal with Tampa Bay that also netted reliever Rick White, who won his first appearance. The Bordick deal, however, would be lamentable. It cost the Mets Melvin Mora, and Bordick scurried back to Baltimore as a free agent after the season was over anyway.

Armando Benitez became the first Met to save forty games in a season. His forty-one saves broke the mark of thirty-eight set by John Franco in 1998, the year before the Mets acquired Benitez. (Franco remained the closer until he injured his finger in July 1999.)

It's not exactly a record, but the sixty-six steals by the 2000 Mets were the same number as 1999 club leader Roger Cendeno (sent to Houston in the Mike Hampton deal). The eight steals by "speedsters" Lenny Harris and Derek Bell were the lowest number for a full-season Mets stolen-bases leader in twenty-five years, when another Met not known for his speed—Dave Kingman—led the 1975 Mets with seven swipes.

Attendance: 2,800,221—Shea's highest since 1989 (and that included losing a home game to open 2000 in Japan).

Indelible Image: Alas, this one is predictable. In a season in which the Mets won a pennant, the war of words and wood lasted far longer than the Mets did in the World Series. The battle began in July when Roger Clemens, tagged for a Mike Piazza grand slam earlier in the summer, drilled the All-Star catcher in the head. Piazza missed the All-Star Game, but he picked up his monster year where he left off. Then in Game 2 of the Series, after Piazza shattered his bat on a Clemens fastball, Rocket picked up the barrel and threw it toward Piazza. Luckily, he missed. The umpires quickly got between the players and no one was ejected, but Clemens beat the Mets, putting them in a two-games-to-none hole they would never climb out of. The simmering feud would continue, but Clemens won the battle that mattered.

2000 Baseball Roundup

NLDS: Mets defeat NL West champ Giants, 3–1.

NLCS: Mets defeat NL Central champion Cardinals, 4–1.

World Series: Yankees defeat Mets, 4–2.

NL MVP: Jeff Kent, Giants.

NL Cy Young: Randy Johnson, Diamondbacks.

NL Rookie of the Year: Rafael Furcal, Braves.

Hall of Fame Inductees: Carlton Fisk, Tony Perez, Sparky Anderson, Bid McPhee, Turkey Stearnes.

Elsewhere

Top News Stories: Florida's hanging chads hold up presidential election outcome for a month; Y2K hysteria turns out to be nothing to worry about—the unforeseen bursting of the dot.com bubble caused harm to far more people.

Top Sports Stories: Recently relocated St. Louis (nee Los Angeles) and Tennessee (nee Houston) play a classic Super Bowl decided by a tackle at the goal line; Tiger Woods becomes the first golfer since 1953 to win three majors in one year; the United States edges Russia, 92–88, for most Olympic medals in Sydney, including the country's only gold for baseball.

Best Picture Winner: *Gladiator.*

Top-Selling U.S. Album: *No Strings Attached* by NSYNC.

Price of Gas: $1.26 (gallon).

Price of a Box Seat at Shea Stadium: $30.

☺ The Rest of the Best: Honorable Mention ☺

2006

What Happened: The Mets set a record for home runs, but the new era of Mets greatness that many thought had arrived began its descent the night that Yadier Molina homered in the ninth inning in Game 7 of the NLCS. David Wright, Carlos Delgado, and Carlos Beltran all had twenty home runs by the All-Star break and the Mets nursed a twelve-game July lead to their first NL East title since 1988. A solid bullpen, fronted by new closer Billy Wagner, covered for an injured and aged rotation as the Mets ended Atlanta's fourteen-year playoff run. After the Mets dispatched the Dodgers in the Division Series, St. Louis ended the Mets' dreams of a world championship as Beltran watched Adam Wainwright's final curve with the tying runs on base.

Mets Valuable Player: There are many to choose from, including reclamation project Jose Valentin at second base; Paul LoDuca, Mike Piazza's replacement behind the plate; and even Duaner Sanchez, whose sterling start to the season helped the Mets build their big lead and whose shoulder injury in a taxi cab in July may have been the difference between reaching the World Series and wondering what might have been. But the MVP of the 2006 team was **Carlos Beltran** (127 runs, 41 homers, 116 RBI), called third strike or not. Beltran was at his best in 2006, quieting the critics who had questioned the first year of his seven-year deal. If he'd only swung at that last pitch.

Attendance: 3,379,535—highest to that point at Shea; first division title or three million attendance figure since 1988.

1988

What Happened: The climax of 2006 was a remake of 1988 with a more dramatic ending—Yadier Molina did a perfect imitation of Mike Scioscia, only he hit a go-ahead instead of a tying ninth-inning homer and did it in Game 7 instead of Game 4. During the 1988 season, the Mets beat the Dodgers in ten of eleven games, but it was turned upside down come October. Orel Hershiser pitched four times in the NLCS, getting the save in Game 4 after Kirk Gibson's homer snapped the tie in the twelfth. The Mets had one of the most dominant pitching staffs in club history, but the equilibrium was thrown off when Bobby Ojeda missed the end of the season following an accident with hedge clippers (one can't help but compare that to the Duaner Sanchez accident in 2006). Agonizing endings like this shouldn't happen to one club twice in a century; it happened to the Mets twice in eighteen years.

Mets Valuable Player: Since **Darryl Strawberry** was robbed of the National League MVP by the Baseball Writers Association, we won't do it to him here. Strawberry led the NL with 39 homers, scored and drove in 101, and led the NL in slugging, OPS, and OPS plus. He split the MVP vote with Kevin McReynolds, who finished third, according to the baseball writers, behind L.A.'s Kirk Gibson. McReynolds was superb in all facets of the game with twenty-seven homers, ninety-nine RBI, a perfect twenty-one-for-twenty-one in steals, and an NL-best seventeen assists in left field. In just his second full season, David Cone went 20-3, 2.22 ERA, 213 strikeouts, and was as good as any pitcher not named "Hershiser."

Attendance: 3,047,724—the highest in Mets history to this point, it remained the standard until the next division-winning season in 2006.

1984

What Happened: We got our lives back, that's what happened. After seven years of finishing fifth or sixth—usually sixth—and losing ninety games every year except for strike-shortened 1981, the Mets improved by twenty-two games in the standings. The Mets held the NL East for sixty-five days before fading to second in August. The Mets would prove they were no fluke, spawning a Mets renaissance that lasted through the decade. Attendance in 1984 improved by more than seven hundred thousand, and the level of fan devotion increased exponentially. First-year manager Davey Johnson knew the organization's young personnel and pushed veterans out of the way to let the kids soar. The 1984 Mets actually allowed fourteen more runs than they scored, yet they won twelve more games than conventional wisdom says they should have (even the 1969 Mets were only eight wins over the Pythagorean projection). And Frank Cashen's front office received the *Baseball America* Organization of the Year for the second season running. The Mets were back. Finally!

Mets Valuable Player: I'd like to say Keith Hernandez, who finished second in the NL MVP voting to Chicago Ryne Sandberg, but the Mets' MVP in 1984 was **Dwight Gooden** (17–9, 2.60 ERA, 276 K's). The nineteen-year-old's arrival changed Shea Stadium as well as the culture surrounding the team. He was an instant ace who immediately rivaled any pitcher in the National League for supremacy. Dominant out of the gate, he would be otherworldly the following year as he cruised to the 1985 Cy Young and Triple Crown. The ninety-win team included young faces brought to New York through shrewd trades (Sid Fernandez, Ron Darling, and Walt Terrell), impeccable drafting (Gooden and Darryl Strawberry), and allowing players from the previous regime to blossom (Mookie Wilson, Hubie Brooks, Wally Backman, and Jesse Orosco).

Attendance: 1,829,482—highest since 1973.

1997

What Happened: Though not as unexpected as 1984, the success of 1997 came on the heels of the false hope of "Generation K"—a season in which prolific offense resulted in ninety-one losses. Bobby Valentine had taken over during the final month in 1996 and started putting his imprint on the team, giving unheralded minor leaguers a chance to contribute and using every player on the roster on an almost-nightly basis. Bernard Gilkey and Lance Johnson did not approach the kind of years they'd enjoyed in 1996, but everyone else stepped up. The Mets competed until the season's final week, winning eighty-eight times, for the club's best record since 1990. In the midst of their success, however, General Manager Joe McIlvaine—one of the few front-office links to the mid-1980s glory days—was pushed out the door in favor of cell-phone savvy Steve Phillips.

Mets Valuable Player: John Olerud came from Toronto in one of the great heists in club history, anchoring the middle of the order as well as the infield. Olerud led the Mets in numerous offensive categories and his three-run homer on the final day of the year pushed him over one hundred RBI. Though he missed time with injuries, catcher Todd Hundley reached thirty homers for the second straight year. Edgardo Alfonzo led the team with a .315 average and was steady at third base. The contributions from these sources might have surprised some, but Rick Reed was a revelation. A former replacement player with no past major-league success, the thirty-two-year-old righty won thirteen times, while allowing scant runs (2.89 ERA) and runners (1.042 per inning) and becoming the team's number-two starter behind Bobby Jones. Dave Mlicki wasn't great, but he did shut out the Yankees in the first regular-season meeting ever between the clubs.

Attendance: 1,766,174 (just tenth of fourteen teams).

2001

What Happened: The encore season to the 2000 National League pennant was surreal. The Mets stumbled out of the gate and stood at 13½ games back in mid-August. They put together a furious comeback . . . and then everything stopped on September 11. Though the world, the city, and the team was distracted, the Mets returned and continued their torrid play. No hit was as big for so many reasons as Mike Piazza's two-run home run that put the Mets ahead in the eighth inning the night that baseball returned to New York on September 21. The comeback stalled a few days later, but the team—like the city—showed its character and resilience. The Mets have had twenty-two seasons with a record as good or better than the 82–80 mark of 2001, but that season meant more—and continues to mean more—due to events away from the ballpark.

Mets Valuable Player: Mike Piazza. Not a surprise given his momentous home run on September 21, but he was the only Met all year to perform close to his peak level. Piazza put together thirty-six home runs and ninety-four RBI, while batting .300 with an OPS plus of 147—numbers no other Mets regular came remotely close to. He won the Silver Slugger and finished in the top fifteen of the MVP voting for the eighth straight year. On a pitching staff where no starter won more than eleven games or had an ERA below Al Leiter's 3.31, Armando Benitez set a club record with forty-three saves. Yet Armando's two late-September blowups against Atlanta—twice wiping out leads forged by Leiter—showed that even emotional fans laid low by world events, could return to their normal passion levels when angered. Life wasn't back to normal, but some feelings were as they'd been.

Attendance: 2,658,279—attendance decreased the year after going to the postseason; also happened in 1974 and 1989.

◯ The Best of the Worst ◯

A brief explanation, the first thing the Mets were known for was being the worst team anyone had ever seen. So stacking up the worst and seeing which gave off the worst odor only makes sense.

Please note that the 1963–1965 teams could easily have made this list, but after 1962, let's just say the rest of the decade gets stamped for "time served"—and we can look at other bad clubs from other eras when more was expected of the franchise. And the 1960s had a pretty groovy ending for Mets fans, anyway.

Table 2.2.   Last-Place Mets Teams

Year	Record	Pct.	GB	Manager(s)
1962	40–120	.250	60½	Stengel
1963	51–111	.315	48½	Stengel
1964	53–109	.327	40	Stengel
1965	50–112	.309	47	Stengel/Westrum
1967	61–101	.377	40½	Westrum/Parker
1977	64–98	.395	37	Torre
1978	66–96	.407	24	Torre
1979	63–99	.389	35	Torre
1982	65–97	.401	27	Bamberger
1983	69–94	.420	22	Bamberger/Howard
1993	59–103	.364	38	Torborg/Green
2002	75–86	.466	26½	Valentine
2003	66–95	.410	34½	Howe

Note: There were ten teams in the National League from 1962 to 1968, six teams in the NL East from 1969 to 1992, seven teams in the NL East in 1993, and five teams in the division since 1994.

1962

How Bad Were They? They were so bad that all terrible teams have since been compared to them . . . and have been found lacking. The only team before them with more losses was the 1899 Cleveland Spiders (20–134), and the only one to threaten them since was the 2003 Detroit Tigers (43–119). The term "1962 Mets" means, "utterly outclassed and bereft of hope"— used in a sentence: "If any club ever surpasses the 1962 Mets for losses it should be automatic cause for contraction."

Flawed Vision: In a vain attempt to draw fans, Mets President George Weiss thought his team needed former Brooklyn Dodgers and New York Giants, in short, anyone old. Mets hitters were among the oldest in the league, and Mets pitchers were among the youngest. Their fielders were the worst regardless of age. The Mets committed a staggering 210 errors and allowed 147 unearned runs on top of allowing 5.04 earned runs per game.

Odd Stat: Somehow, the 1962 Mets drew more walks than did any other team in the National League. Exactly 616 times, a manager kicked a step when his pitcher walked an original Met. The 1962 Mets even defied the importance of getting on base—though they did score twenty-five more times (and lose twenty-four more times) than did their fellow expansion club, the Houston Colt .45s.

Signature Moment of Ineptitude: How much time have you got? Jimmy Breslin's 1963 classic *Can't Anybody Here Play This Game,* taken from a Casey Stengel quote, made the Mets a household name. Stengel, Breslin, the press, and the fans, all played it for laughs. The biggest guffaws surrounded "Marvelous Marv" Throneberry, with the best line coming when he was called out on a two-run triple for missing first base. When Stengel came out to argue, first-base coach Cookie Lavagetto cautioned him: "Forget it Casey, he missed second, too."

Attendance: 922,530—only one other time in half a century did the Mets draw under one million in a full season (1979). See why below.

Aging Ungracefully: 1962

Average Age of 1962 Mets: 28.6 Years.
Average Time with Mets after 1962: 1.2 Years.
Average Time in Majors after 1962: 2.3 Years.
Note: These numbers include 1962 callup Ed Kranepool, who spent seventeen more seasons with the Mets.

1977

How Bad Were They? They were so bad they traded Tom Seaver and killed any incentive to be a Mets fan until 1984. On June 15, the same day they dealt Seaver for four Reds prospects, the Mets also shipped out surly slugger Dave Kingman to San Diego. More trades of recognizable names followed. Whereas the Mets had previously sent away the likes of Amos Otis, Nolan Ryan, Rusty Staub, and Tug McGraw in the misguided belief that these deals would make them better, the Mets traded in 1977 to get rid of players ownership did not want to negotiate with or pay. You could not laugh away the losing or the ineptitude, like fans had in the 1960s. This was the low point in franchise history.

Flawed Vision: Mets Chairman M. Donald Grant had negotiated a three-year, $775,000 deal (plus incentives) with Tom Seaver a year earlier. Grant took the ruling that brought free agency to baseball as almost a personal affront. Grant not only refused to revisit Seaver's contract, he also insulted his star player publicly and used columnist Dick Young to attack Seaver on a daily basis in the *Daily News*. When Seaver went over Grant's head to owner Lorinda de Roulet for a contract extension that would have kept "The Franchise" in Flushing through 1981, an inflammatory Young column appeared the day of the trade deadline that made Seaver's past promise to the owner null and void. Seaver demanded a trade and got it.

Odd Stat: The three Mets who tied for the club lead in home runs with twelve—Steve Henderson, John Milner, and John Stearns—combined to still finish one home run below the thirty-seven that Dave Kingman hit the previous year to lead the Mets. And that was with Kong missing a month with a thumb injury in 1976. Home runs weren't all that was missing from the 1977 Mets.

Signature Moment of Ineptitude: The lights were turned out on the Mets literally and symbolically in 1977. Unlike other parts of the city during the July 13 blackout, Shea was calm and orderly when all went dark in the midst of a Mets-Cubs game. At least the Mets couldn't lose that night (they'd lose the continuation of the game in September). And in the light of day on August 21, Tom Seaver returned to Shea wearing a Reds uniform before a full house. Even the most diehard Mets fans pulled for Tom to be terrific that day. He was, of course. Seaver beat his old buddy, Jerry Koosman, who would lose twenty games after winning twenty in 1976. Joe Torre, the first Mets player directly hired to manage, could only wonder what he'd gotten himself into.

Attendance: 1,066,825—the smallest number at Shea to that point, in the twelve-year-old park's existence.

1979

How Bad Were They? They were so bad they admitted as much. After acquiring 1–6 Dock Ellis and Andy Hassler, he of the 8.80 ERA, at the trading deadline, General Manager Joe McDonald uttered the cryptic remark: "If their records were super, we wouldn't have obtained them." And this from a team that used all manner of beasts of burden at Shea Stadium. The Mets paraded a mule named "Mettle" on the field before games, riding in a surrey driven by one of owner Lorinda de Roulet's daughters or a "lucky" grounds crew member.

Flawed Vision: The owner made one last stab at putting together a team that could at least not lose so much money (winning was out of the question). Charles Shipman Payson, the widower of the team's matriarch, Joan Payson, who died in 1975, seemingly had his mind made up to sell the Mets before the club even took the field at Shea Stadium before the smallest crowd ever to see a Shea opener (10,406). Among the few in attendance was M. Donald Grant, though no longer in an official capacity. The eight-person board of directors had relieved Grant of his duties the previous November. As the late 1970s pop duet of Johnny Mathis and Deniece Williams intoned, "Too Much, Too Little, Too Late."

Odd Stat: In the tenth anniversary season of the one-hundred-win world championship club that shocked the world in 1969, the 1979 Mets needed their own version of a miracle—they pieced together a season-ending, six-game winning streak to avoid the century mark in losses. The Mets, who had endured two nine-game losing streaks in the previous month (including being swept in four successive doubleheaders at home), were one out away from loss number one hundred at Wrigley Field in the second game of yet another twinbill on September 25. Richie Hebner, who spent his year as a Met behaving as if he were serving out a sentence in a chain gang, singled in the tying run against Cy Young–winner Bruce Sutter. Steve Henderson knocked in the winning run an inning later, and the Mets won out to finish at 63–99.

Signature Moment of Ineptitude: After the Mets tied the eventual world champion Pirates with two outs in the ninth at Shea Stadium on May 25, Joel Youngblood led off the bottom of the eleventh with a high flyball to left that Bill Robinson never saw in the dense Flushing fog. By the time Robinson retrieved the ball, Youngblood was at third base. The umpires pulled the teams off the field, and the game was called by fog. Instead of the Mets having a man at third and none out, the game was declared a tie and was restarted from scratch as part of a doubleheader. On August 25, the Mets won a game, but Pete Falcone lost a shutout when Ed Kranepool, thinking the game was already over because of a controversial umpire ruling, was in the clubhouse instead of at first base when the last out was made. When the teams arrived the next day, they were told they had to get that last out. The batter was retired—officially—but it did cost Falcone the complete game. A minor irritation in a season of major ones, it was the team's only win in a thirteen-game stretch.

Attendance: 788,905—the smallest full-season attendance in Mets history (though the 1981 Mets drew 86,995 fewer fans in a season shortened by two months due to a strike).

1993

How Bad Were They? They became the only Mets team since the 1960s to lose one hundred games, and the club finished behind a first-year expansion team to boot. These Mets are the only team in the history of the National League East to finish seventh. (The division, grown one larger by the Florida Marlins, was reduced to five clubs in 1994.)

Flawed Vision: The Mets refused to see the iceberg in front of them. They began the year infuriated by the publication of *The Worst Team Money Could Buy*, which highlighted their dysfunctional 1992 season, but all the 1993 Mets proved was that the book's title was premature. They were stocked with a roster that included Eddie Murray, Bret Saberhagen, Jeff Kent, Todd Hundley, Tony Fernandez, Vince Coleman, Bobby Bonilla, plus a few remaining 1986 Mets who survived the team's purge in the late 1980s and were now on the downside of their careers. The 1993 Mets were unwatchable, unlikable, and unbearable. Both the manager and general manager (Jeff Torborg and Al Harazin) were fired during the season and replaced by Dallas Green and Joe McIlvaine.

Odd Stat: Sticking out amid a sea of land mines was Anthony Young's major league record twenty-seven-game losing streak. It began on April

19, 1992, and ended on July 28, 1993, when the Mets actually bailed him out with a walkoff win after he was in line to lose number twenty-eight in a row. Young worked as a starter, closer, and middle reliever, but no matter where he pitched, the Mets found a way to lose behind him—though he picked up sixteen saves during his skein. Young broke the mark of nineteen straight losses, set in the 1960s by Craig Anderson, who surpassed the mark of eighteen, set by Roger Craig. Both pitchers were Mets, of course.

Signature Moment of Ineptitude: Vince Coleman tossing a lit firecracker at a group of people after a game in Los Angeles and injuring three, including a toddler. Coleman, who'd injured Dwight Gooden earlier in the year swinging a golf club in the clubhouse, never played for the Mets again. *This moment in Mets ineptitude presented by Clorox, the bleach that Bret Saberhagen prefers to spray at reporters.*

Attendance: 1,873,183—actually an increase over 1992, but the Mets would not surpass this figure again until 1998.

2009

How Bad Were They? They were so bad that they stunk up a brand new stadium and didn't leave any identifying marks on the building, so no one could tell who played there—sort of like not leaving a note on the windshield after backing into someone's car in a parking lot.

Flawed Vision: After losing a heartbreaker in the 2006 NLCS, followed by successive soul-crushing endings in 2007 and 2008, in which the Mets fell out of first place in September and finished one game out of a playoff spot, the Mets continued to look behind rather than ahead. General Manager Omar Minaya tried to fix the previous year's problem (the bullpen), while failing to upgrade an offense that could not score in the big new ballpark. The bullpen wasn't much better than it had been, and the rest of the team was worse, when it wasn't injured—the Mets had twenty-two different disabled-list stints.

Odd Stat: The Mets tied with the Dodgers for the league lead with a .270 batting average. Yet the Mets were last in the majors—by a lot—with just ninety-five homers, the fewest by the club since the 1992 *Worst Team Money Could Buy* club. Again, that name seems to have been awarded prematurely.

Signature Moment of Ineptitude: Nineteen different Mets teams have lost ninety or more games, but this club was special. When their director of scouting wasn't tearing off his shirt to "motivate" minor leaguers, the GM was accusing a reporter of slanting his stories to try to get a job with the dysfunctional organization. The moment that cannot be erased, however, is the dropped pop-up by Luis Castillo that allowed the tying and winning runs to cross home plate in the team's first visit to the new Yankee Stadium. And then the Mets were swept by the Yankees a few weeks later in their first visit to Citi Field. Talk about convivial hosts.

Attendance: 3,154,262—represents a near-capacity crowd per night but was nearly 900,000 less than they drew for the last year at Shea in 2008.

☺ The Rest of the Worst: Dishonorable Mention ☺

1967

Bad to the Bone: After avoiding 100 losses for the first time and showing real progress in 1966, Wes Westrum's 1967 club regressed: they hit 101 in the "L" column and required a complete overhaul. It wasn't as if GM Bing Devine wasn't already changing on the fly—he went through a record fifty-four players, including twenty-seven pitchers. The media, fans, and those just trying to keep their scorecards straight were getting impatient with the Mets. Would they ever get better?

Hope on the Horizon? Two years later, the Mets were world champions, but no one had any inkling of that during the "Summer of Love." Though the team still couldn't hit and the pitching in general left a lot to be desired, any year with Tom Seaver as Rookie of the Year has some redeeming qualities. The 1967 debacle also led to the hiring of Gil Hodges, and that worked out pretty well.

Attendance: 1,565,492—being in New York has its advantages; the Mets were fourth in the majors—nine clubs drew under one million.

1982

Bad to the Bone: By George, this year had nothing going for it. George Foster came from the Reds in a big deal and had a big bust of a year. George Bamberger, meanwhile, made one realize that Joe Torre, who would go on to win the 1982 NL West crown in his first year in Atlanta, might have been a little better skipper than Mets fans gave him credit for. What hurt about 1982 at Shea was that the Mets were actually in the thick of things—briefly. The Mets were six games over .500 heading into June—unheard of at the time. From that point on, the Mets averaged exactly one win for every three games and embarked on the worst road trip to that point in club history (0–9) and a fifteen-game losing skid, second only to the 1962 Mets.

Hope on the Horizon? Believe it or not, the club that lost ninety-seven games with unerring precision would win ninety games just two years later. Of course, many of the players—plus the wishy-washy manager—would be gone by then. Thank God.

Attendance: 1,320,055—lured by the "By George" PR campaign and a fast start, this was Shea's highest attendance figure since 1976, the year before they dealt Tom Seaver.

1978

Bad to the Bone: It was Joe Torre's first full season as a manager, and the team was an utter mess—better than 1977 or 1979, mind you, but Mets management continued to be delusional. While other teams went out and signed big-time free agents like Rich Gossage (Yankees), Mike Torrez (Red Sox), and Larry Hisle (Brewers), the Mets signed their first free agent ever: minor league pitcher Tom Hausman. The same day the Cubs signed former Mets slugger Dave Kingman, the Mets inked injury-prone utility man Elliot Maddox. The bad times kept on coming.

Hope on the Horizon? No. None whatsoever. Even with league ERA leader Craig Swan (2.43), the Mets still finished tenth of twelve National League teams in ERA (and last in adjusted ERA). According to Wins Above Replacement, Swan and catcher John Stearns were worth almost eleven wins between them, putting them among the league's best. The rest of the team wasn't worth much, accumulating just sixty-six wins that mattered and ninety-six losses, the most in the National League.

Attendance: 1,007,328—only Pete Rose's hit streak reaching thirty-nine at Shea helped the Mets sneak over a million.

2003

Bad to the Bone: The Mets quit on Bobby Valentine in 2002, and the Mets fired the popular and volatile manager after his only losing campaign in six full seasons with the club. General Manager Steve Phillips, somehow kept on after the 2002 debacle, picked Art Howe, who set an American League record with twenty straight wins and a third straight division title, yet the A's were only too happy to let him come to New York to manage. The team took advantage of the pleasant—and overwhelmed—babysitter and lost ninety-five games, even as Steve Trachsel and Al Leiter won sixteen and fifteen games, respectively. Big free-agent signee Tom Glavine (9–14) realized he wasn't in Georgia anymore.

Hope on the Horizon? On the plus side, the Mets did finally get rid of Steve Phillips and unloaded numerous onerous contracts, but new GM Jim Duquette didn't get anyone of lasting value in return. The Mets showed promise in 2004 but overreached and fell flat.

Attendance: 2,187,291—sounds like an awful lot of people going to see this dreck, but the inflated attendance figures left the Mets only eleventh in the league.

1992

Bad to the Bone: While a $44.5 million payroll today might not even cover the salaries of a pitching staff, that sum brought New York some of the game's biggest names—empty names it turned out, who looked good on paper and bad in a book. *The Worst Team Money Could Buy* by beat writers Bob Klapisch and John Harper showed that the team was as unlikable as it was dysfunctional. David Cone was dealt, John Franco was hurt, Bobby

Bonilla flopped, Vince Coleman whined, and Anthony Young lost and lost and lost. Former American League Manager of the Year Jeff Torborg, wooed from the White Sox, could not handle the team or the press. They deserved to lose more than just ninety games—more disappointment.

Hope on the Horizon? The next year, the team lost 103 games and the only players left by 1997, when the Mets had their next winning season, were Todd Hundley and John Franco, who missed all of July and September 1992. So, 1992 was an utter waste, and the team didn't get better until most of the roster had been purged.

Attendance: 1,779,534—and every one of them should have gotten their money back.

Mets People

Karl Ehrhardt: "The Sign Man"

Anyone can second-guess managers, players, and coaches, but no one ever said it from the stands quite like Shea Stadium's Sign Man. Karl Ehrhardt was a fixture at Shea for the first seventeen years of its existence. He sat in a coworker's box seat down the third-base line and held up directly-to-the-point block-letter signs, from a collection he kept at the ready. He was the first to call Shea "Grant's Tomb" in the 1960s—a reference to the stingy Mets chairman M. Donald Grant—and yet Ehrhardt was invited by the team to show his stuff in Oakland during the 1973 World Series. Fans loved him, as did the Channel 9 cameramen, and the Sign Man received more praise than pans from the players he sometimes skewered.

There was plenty of competition. Banners were a crucial part of the Mets fan identity from the club's earliest days in 1962. If someone was going to become involved with a 120-loss team, they wanted everyone to know why. Banners were a hit, especially with Manager Casey Stengel. General Manager George Weiss eventually saw the light and stopped having the homemade signs confiscated. The Mets initiated Banner Day at the Polo Grounds in 1963 and held it as an annual on-field parade at Shea for more than three decades. So what made the Sign Man so special?

First of all, he was a professional. Ehrhardt was a commercial artist who sat in Section 72E on Tuesdays and Fridays from 1965 to 1981. The one-time Brooklyn Dodgers rooter gave himself over completely to the new National League team in town. He was instantly recognizable in his crushed Mets derby, and his signs spoke for themselves. "Look Ma, No Hands" might come up after an error or "Can You Believe It?" when the Mets pulled off the unexpected in a positive way. His handiwork was pictured in *Life* magazine in 1969: "Toothless Cubs Just a Lotta Lip." His most famous sign came a few weeks later when the Mets had incredibly run past the Cubs, Braves, and Orioles, in that order. As the field filled with championship revelers on October 16, 1969, Ehrhardt held a sign aloft that simply said, "There Are No Words." Manager Gil Hodges had kind words for him at Gracie Mansion after the victory parade: "I just want to thank you for your contributions to the team."

By 1981, he had twelve hundred signs and spent hours in his garage deciding which thirty or forty foldable signs to bring with him. That was his last year as a fixture at Shea. In one of his last interviews before his death at age eighty-three in 2008, he told writer Charlie Vascellaro, in *Shea 1964–2008*, that he got into a heated dispute with a Mets official about not being invited to an event that he'd always attended. He returned twenty-one years later at the team's invitation for the fortieth anniversary of Mets baseball.

There have been countless others who have held up signs at Mets games, including some—like Sal Candiano—who have done so faithfully through good times and bad. Anyone around the Mets in the 1960s and 1970s, however, will tell you that there was only one Sign Man. And he spoke for everyone.

C H A P T E R

3

Best Mets Games

IGHT OFF THE BAT, we may have a disagreement. When it comes to a team that's famous for *not* getting the job done, the top spots go to the games where the Mets got it done, got to celebrate, and etched their name on the big trophy. The rest is pretty self-explanatory. You'll agree with some, disagree with others—that's how these things work.

☺ Top-Ten Games, Postseason ☺

1. October 27, 1986: Mets 8, Red Sox 5—World Series Game 7

With the marbles on the table, the Mets came through—the 108-win team acting like the underdog, as they did throughout the World Series. Bruce Hurst, with two of Boston's three wins (and prematurely declared Series MVP, just before the Mets' epic comeback in Game 6), got the start in the decisive game after a rainout enabled the Sox to alter their rotation. Ron Darling, also starting for the third time in the Series, was not sharp and Boston took a 3–0 lead. Though Sid Fernandez came out of the pen and kept the Mets in the ballgame, Hurst blanked the Mets through 5⅓ innings. Two hits and a walk loaded the bases for Keith Hernandez, who singled home two runs and put the tying run on third. Gary Carter then tied the game. After Roger McDowell set down the Sox in the seventh, Series MVP

101

Ray Knight homered to give the Mets the lead, and Rafael Santana and Hernandez knocked in runs that proved big when Boston knocked out McDowell with two runs in the eighth. Jesse Orosco came in to save the day and then singled in the bottom of the inning for an insurance run. Marty Barrett, who had struck out only once while setting a record with thirteen World Series hits, went down swinging and Orosco's glove went flying. For the ages.

2. October 15, 1969: Mets 5, Orioles 3—World Series Game 5

You never forget your first. The clincher shares a common theme with many of the greatest Mets October moments: It started with things looking pretty bad for the Mets. Two third-inning home runs off Jerry Koosman put the Mets in a 3–0 hole with a return trip to Baltimore in the offing if they couldn't finish off the Orioles. The Mets had done little against Dave McNally until a pitch near Cleon Jones's feet bounced into the Mets dugout. Manager Gil Hodges emerged with a ball with shoe polish on it, and Jones was sent to first. Donn Clendenon followed with his third home run of the World Series (and gained Series MVP). Al Weis, who had never homered at Shea Stadium, did so in the seventh to even the game. Ron Swoboda's double snapped the tie in the eighth, and the Mets got an insurance run on an O's "E." It was left to Koosman, but he walked the leadoff batter. He retired Boog Powell and Brooks Robinson before Davey Johnson lifted one to deep left that Kooz initially thought was a home run. Cleon didn't. He caught the ball and bent on a knee as countless prayers were answered. The Miracle of Flushing was complete. The Mets were world champions. No pigs were seen flying, but countless streams of ticker tape flew indeed.

3. October 25, 1986: Mets 6, Red Sox 5—World Series Game 6

This is the most memorable game on the list, and why not? It began with a rogue parachutist landing on the field and ended with a trickling ground ball. After a frigid 1–0 Red Sox win in the opener, the team that won each of the next four games had leads of four or more runs. Game 6, on the other hand, was back and forth throughout. The Red Sox scored in each of the first two innings, including a two-out Dwight Evans RBI double minutes after Michael Sergio landed on the field. The Mets tied the Red Sox in the fifth, but Boston took the lead in the seventh. After the Red Sox batted for Roger Clemens in the top of the eighth, the Mets tied it in the bottom of the inning on Gary Carter's sacrifice fly that was set up when reliever Calvin Schiraldi was late throwing to second on a bunt. The Red Sox took the lead in the tenth on Dave Henderson's home run, followed by a Marty Barrett run-scoring single off Rick Aguilera. The Mets were down to their last out when Carter, Kevin Mitchell, and Ray Knight all singled to knock out ex-Met Schiraldi and bring in Bob Stanley to face Mookie Wilson. First, Mookie jackknifed out of the way of a wild pitch that let the tying run score; he then fouled off six pitches in a row before putting the ball in fair territory toward Bill Buckner. As broadcaster Vin Scully saw it, "It's a little roller up along first—behind the bag! Here comes Knight and the Mets win it!" Win it they did.

4. October 15, 1986: Mets 7, Astros 6—NLCS Game 6

For sheer thrills and drama, Jerry Izenberg has a point with his book title about this contest, *The Greatest Game Ever Played*. The Astros scored three times off Bobby Ojeda in the first inning, but Ojeda allowed nothing more for the next four innings; Rick Aguilera was superb in three innings of work. Lenny Dykstra opened the ninth with a pinch-hit triple to spark a three-run rally, and Ray Knight tied the game on a sacrifice fly against Dave Smith. Roger McDowell tossed five shutout innings in relief and was matched by Houston's bullpen until the fourteenth inning, when the Mets scratched out a run on a Wally Backman single. With the Mets having held Houston scoreless for thirteen straight innings, Billy Hatcher hit the foul pole against Jesse Orosco to tie the game once more. With the game having become the longest postseason game to that point in history, the Mets appeared to break it open in the sixteenth inning on RBI hits by Knight and Dykstra sandwiched around a run-scoring wild pitch. Orosco, pitching his fifth inning of relief in just over twenty-four hours, got the first out before allowing a walk and successive singles. Keith Hernandez aggressively went for the force on a groundout, which became a game-saver when Glenn Davis followed with a single that would have scored two instead of one. Hernandez threatened to fight catcher Gary Carter if he called another fastball, and Orosco's big curve got Kevin Bass swinging to clinch the pennant.

5. October 11, 1986: Mets 6, Astros 5—NLCS Game 3

The Mets got the upper hand in the series by winning the team's first postseason game at Shea Stadium in thirteen years, but it looked like a downer early on when the Astros took a 4–0 lead. After an error and a three-run home run by Darryl Strawberry tied it in the sixth, a Ray Knight miscue the following inning put the Astros back on top. Dave Smith came on to try to close out the game in the ninth, but the inning began with a drag bunt by Wally Backman, who lunged across the bag safely—though the Astros legitimately questioned whether Backman was out of the baseline. After Backman took second on a wild pitch, Danny Heep flied out to short center. Up came Lenny Dykstra, who hadn't even started the game. Dykstra, with just nine home runs in 232 major league games to that point, slammed a drive into the Mets bullpen as Shea erupted and "Nails" leapt his way around the bases.

6. October 17, 1999: Mets 4, Braves 3—NLCS Game 5

When is a walkoff home run not a walkoff home run? When it's a grand slam single. Though this game represents the only postseason series on the list that the Mets eventually lost, this game remains one of the most memorable contests in club history. John Olerud had homered—back when it was dry—in the first inning. And the Mets did not score for the next thirteen innings, as the sun went down and a steady drizzle enveloped Shea Stadium. The Mets weathered the storm, so to speak, using nine pitchers to strand nineteen Braves on the bases, but Keith Lockhart, who'd been thrown out at the plate by Melvin Mora to end the thirteenth inning, tripled in the go-ahead run in the top of the fifteenth off rookie Octavio Dotel. With the Braves needing three outs to clinch the pennant, Shawon Dunston fouled off six 3–2 pitches before singling and stealing second. Rookie Kevin McGlinchy walked two batters—one intentionally following a sacrifice—before walking Todd Pratt to force in the tying run. McGlinchy got the ball over the plate to Robin Ventura, who crushed it through the mist and into the bullpen. But Pratt, whose home run had touched off a wild celebration a week earlier, instigated an even crazier moment when he turned to embrace Ventura, who thereby passed the runner Pratt, negating the grand slam. The winning run had crossed home plate, and the "grand slam single" became part of postseason lore.

7. October 8, 1999: Mets 4, Diamondbacks 3—NLDS Game 4

A grueling finish to the 1999 season saw the Mets go from Wild Card shoo-in to roadkill in a frightening ten-day span. The Mets rallied the final weekend of the season to force a one-game playoff and win the Wild Card in game 163 in Cincinnati. Mike Piazza caught all but one inning during the previous sixteen games, including the last nine games with no days off and every game a must-win. Piazza wasn't just tired, he was hurting—his left thumb was so swollen after Game 2 that he could not swing a bat or put on a glove. Todd Pratt took over behind the plate against the Diamond-backs as the Mets took a two-games-to-one series lead. Pratt caught the next afternoon's seesaw battle, which would determine whether the Mets won the series or flew to Phoenix to face Randy Johnson the next day. The Mets blew a lead in the top of the eighth, and then the Diamondbacks let the Mets tie it in the bottom of the inning on a pair of long flyballs, one of which should have been caught. Pratt, whose biggest contribution had been slapping a tag on Jay Bell to keep Arizona's fourth run off the board, came up with one out in the tenth against closer Matt Mantei, who'd come in to face Pratt in the eighth and had retired him with runners at the corners. Now Pratt sent a long drive to center. Gold Glover Steve Finley seemed to have a bead on it as the ball kept carrying. He leaped, looked in his glove, and . . . nothing was there. The stadium erupted; Pratt's fist was punching the air as he rounded the bases. It was just the fourth series-ending home run in postseason history—and the first ever by an understudy.

8. October 12, 1969: Mets 2, Orioles 1—World Series Game 2

It's Amazin' how quickly you can run out of room in a list like this. Games 3 and 4 of the 1969 World Series featured the miraculous Tommie Agee catches, Ron Swoboda's sprawling snag, a ten-inning win by Tom Seaver, and J. C. Martin's wrist deflecting a throw to bring in the winning run. But would all that have happened without Jerry Koosman's building up the club's confidence and evening the Series in Game 2? After the Orioles beat up Tom Seaver in the opener, the naysayers who had the Mets pegged as chicken feed for the Birds were crowing. Kooz shut them all up. He took a no-hitter into the seventh inning before allowing two Baltimore hits and a steal to tie the game at 1–1. Al Weis stroked a two-out single to give the Mets the lead in the ninth. Koosman got the first two outs in the bottom of the inning before walking two straight. Ron Taylor came in to get the final out, and now the team that had been a 100-1 preseason underdog to win the World Series was tied up with the mighty Orioles and heading to Shea—where Kooz would dominate the O's again.

9. October 21, 1986: Mets 7, Red Sox 1—World Series Game 3

Much like 1969, the Mets looked to be in big trouble in this World Series. The difference was that these Mets were favored, and they were down two games to none and just starting on the road portion of the World Series. No matter, the Mets put four on the board in the first inning at Fenway Park, and southpaw Bobby Ojeda cruised against his old Red Sox teammates. A day after Manager Davey Johnson told his club to stiff the press and not even show up at Fenway Park for a planned workout, the Mets worked over Boston. Dykstra had four hits, including a leadoff home run that lit a spark under the team. It was a whole different Series from that night on.

10. October 8, 2000: Mets 4, Giants 0—NLDS Game 4

Bobby Jones rarely got his due as a Mets pitcher. Jones had fronted the mediocre Mets teams of the mid-1990s, but once the Mets got competitive and beefed up their rotation, Jones got lost in the shuffle. He even accepted a demotion to the minors for a few weeks in 2000 to work on mechanics. He was a different pitcher upon his return, but no one saw this coming. The afternoon following a rousing thirteen-inning win against the Giants that gave New York the lead in the NLDS, the Mets needed length, at the very least, from Jones. They got that, as well as everything else the right-hander had. Jones allowed base runners in only one inning. He allowed a double to NL MVP Jeff Kent and a pair of walks, but when Dusty Baker sent up pitcher Mark Gardner with the bases full, Jones did not waste the gift He retired him plus the final dozen batters, for good measure. Of the team's nearly three dozen one-hitters, his is the only one in the postseason.

Rivalries Come, Rivalries Go: Best Rivalry by Decade

The best definition for "rivalry" as it pertains to baseball is "competition for the same objective or for superiority in the same field." With interleague play starting in 1997, teams in other leagues were designated as "rivals" so that teams would have opponents they could play every year, build up some kind of enmity, and thus increase attendance. In the case of the Yankees-Mets rivalry, it has worked, even though the Yankees dominated the first-fifteen season series 7–2–6 (it was extended to have a home series annually in both the Bronx and Flushing in 1999).

The best rivals, though, are division rivals. But those rivals can change, as has been the case with the Mets. The Mets have no true rival but, rather, a series of changing enemies. Some of that was forced on them when the realignment of divisions in 1994 took away three regular foes and transplanted them to the Central Division—so, those old rivalries tend to simmer rather than boil. Reinstating two extra series against division rivals in 2001 helped jump-start some rivalries, while familiarity breeds contempt in others: "They're playing the Marlins? Again!"

Here's a look at the best in rivalries in the first five decades of Mets baseball.

1960s: Chicago Cubs

The Mets did the Cubs a favor early on. While Chicago was struggling through its ridiculous "College of Coaches" period, the Mets were there to act as a buffer from the cold, hard basement. The Cubs had their first 100-loss season ever, dating back to the franchise's founding in the 1870s. And yet the 1962 Cubs finished eighteen games ahead of the Mets. Chicago returned the favor in 1966, losing 103 again and becoming the first team to finish behind the Mets. The ten-team league became two six-team divisions in 1969, with the Mets and Cubs placed in the NL East with the Pittsburgh Pirates, Philadelphia Phillies, St. Louis Cardinals, and first-year Montreal Expos. The Mets rallied from ten games behind Chicago in mid-August to take the division and go on to win the World Series. Though the rivalry is long dormant in New York, the wound from 1969 is still fresh in Chicago. Decade Record vs. Rival: 65–79–1

1970s: Pittsburgh Pirates

To younger fans, the concept of the Pirates either being in the NL East or a dominant club may seem odd, but it's the honest truth. After the Mets won the 1969 division title, the Pirates won the NL East in 1970, 1971, 1972, 1974, and 1975. You'll note one year is not listed: 1973. That year the Mets were in last place at the end of August while the Pirates were in first, but the Mets clawed their way back with a brilliant run. The Mets knocked off the Bucs four times in five days in late September, including the fabled "Ball on the Wall" game. With the Mets free-falling, the Bucs won twenty-five of thirty-six in 1977–1978, but even as the Pirates won ninety-eight and the Mets lost ninety-nine in 1979, the Mets were one fogged-out game at Shea—the game ending in a tie after the umps called it with the winning run at third and none out for the Mets in extra innings—from splitting the season series with the eventual world champs. Decade Record vs. Rival: 78–98–1

1980s: St. Louis Cardinals

Of all these rivalries, this was the most fun. The Cardinals won three pennants and a world championship during the decade. The Mets won two division titles and one World Series, but the chase is what stands out. The Mets needed to win three straight in St. Louis in the final week of 1985 to forge a tie. The Mets won the first two and . . . . The Mets and Cards were neck and neck in September 1987 with a series at Shea and a season-ending set in St. Louis, but Terry Pendleton came up in the ninth with the Cardinals trailing at Shea and . . . . The 1986 NL East title was all but sealed in April when the Mets won four straight at Busch. But a one-game difference in record

Tommie Agee: great Mets center fielder and 1969 World Series hero. *Courtesy of Dwayne Labakas Collection*

From his first year in New York, Tom Seaver was "The Franchise." *Courtesy of Dwayne Labakas Collection*

Ed Kranepool smiles during 1969 season, the eighth season of the Mets and his eighth season. *From the author's collection*

Outspoken outfielder and 1969 World Series hero Ron Swoboda would later become a broadcaster. *From the author's collection*

Bud Harrelson batted more times than any Met other than Ed Kranepool. *Courtesy of Jacob Kanarak*

Classic Jerry Koosman leg kick from the mid-1970s. *Courtesy of Jacob Kanarak*

Fans thronged wherever Dwight Gooden was in the 1980s. Here, he makes a spring training warm-up session into an event. *Courtesy of Dan Carubia*

Ralph Kiner, Bob Murphy, and Lindsey Nelson were together longer than any other broadcasting trio in baseball history. *Courtesy of Dan Carubia*

Mookie Wilson at spring training in Port St. Lucie in 1988, the year new spring digs opened. *Courtesy of Dan Carubia*

Mets ace David Cone getting ready to warm up before a game in Chicago's Wrigley Field. *Courtesy of Dan Carubia*

Jeff Kent: one of the many that got away in one-sided trades. The Mets thought they were getting the best in the 1996 deal with Cleveland for Carlos Baerga. Wrong! *Courtesy of Dan Carubia*

The arrival of Mike Piazza in 1998 signified a tectonic shift in perception and performance in Flushing. *Courtesy of Dan Carubia*

Mr. Met is as popular as any mascot—or any Met. *From the author's collection*

In the second year of Citi Field, the Mets erected a museum and team Hall of Fame in the Jackie Robinson Rotunda to honor Mets history. *From the author's collection*

The new ballpark in Flushing, just like Ebbets Field in Brooklyn—only without so many Dodgers fans. *From the author's collection*

The first year at the ballpark—as night sets, Gary Sheffield bats in August 2009. *Courtesy of Dan Carubia*

over ten years? That's tight. Plus, St. Louis gave away superstar Keith Hernandez to the Mets. This great rivalry can still flare up even from different divisions, notably during the NLCS in 2000 (win) and 2006 (let's not go there).
Decade Record vs. Rival: 87–86

1990s: Atlanta Braves

This was a rivalry only in the papers and on sports-talk radio. You can't have a rivalry where one team dominates the other in every respect. The decade started innocently enough with the Braves in last place in the NL West, but the divisions realigned in 1994, and St. Louis, Chicago, and Pittsburgh were shipped to the Central (just when the Pirates stopped contending). In came the Braves, three years into their fourteen-year run of division titles. Great. Thanks. It's surprising the record for this decade is as close as this, but it does not include Atlanta's 4–2 mark over the Mets in the 1999 NLCS.
Decade Record vs. Rival: 50–69

2000s: Philadelphia Phillies

This actually reflects 2000–2011, and is pretty close, but the Phillies have generally managed to beat the Mets as needed since 2007. If the Mets had won one more game against Philadelphia that year, the 1964 Phillies would still own the greatest collapse in history (at least until the 2011 Boston and Atlanta flops). The 2008 Mets rebounded to go 11–7 against the Phillies, but they blew a 7–0 lead in a late-August game in Philly, lost two of three at Shea, and finished second in both the NL East and the Wild Card. This is the lone Mets rivalry in which proximity plays a factor, and there is no love lost. Through history, the teams have rarely been good at the same time—and Phillies fans no longer even consider the Mets their primary rival.
Decade-Plus Record vs. Rival: 102–114

⚾ Most Heartbreaking Mets Losses, Postseason ⚾

We'll keep this list to five games, for the sanity of all. But Mets fans know from cruel experience it's better to have hoped and lost in the postseason than never to have hoped at all. It does make for a long winter, though.

1. October 26, 2000: Yankees 4, Mets 2—World Series Game 5

When taken with the extra-inning Game-1 loss, the Game-2 Roger Clemens bat fling at Mike Piazza, and the Civil War–like quality that a Mets-Yankees World Series brought to the region, there has never been a more agonizing October finale in Mets history. With a chance to give Mets fans the ultimate bragging rights, the team came up short. Al Leiter, whose win was tossed back in Game 1 by shoddy base running and closer Armando Benitez, held onto the ball in Game 5 until he literally had nothing left. By then light-hitting Luis Sojo had dribbled a ball up the middle on Leiter's 142nd-and-final pitch to snap a 2–2 tie in the ninth. With two outs in the bottom of the frame, Mike Piazza came up as the tying run against Mariano Rivera, but his flyball died in center field—and so did a little bit of every Mets fan. The Yankees—and their fans—celebrating a championship in Flushing? Shea it ain't so.

2. October 19, 1999: Braves 10, Mets 9—NLCS Game 6

Only losing the World Series to the Yankees at home could trump this. The Mets were trying to become the first team to win a postseason series after being down three games to none. But it was not to be. It was an excruciating ending to a great comeback against a hated rival at a place where the Mets never won. The Braves went up 5–0 in the first inning at Turner Field, but Bobby Valentine's club never gave up. After cutting it to 5–3 in the sixth, the Braves tacked on two more runs only to see the Mets score four in the seventh, with Mike Piazza's two-run home run off John Smoltz tying the game. The Mets twice forged a one-run lead, only to see both John Franco and Armando Benitez give it back—that was still preferable to what Kenny Rogers did. He walked Andruw Jones with the bases loaded in the eleventh to send the Braves to the World Series. There was no consolation in Atlanta getting swept by the Yankees.

3. October 19, 2006: Cardinals 3, Mets 1—NLCS Game 7

Hitting had brought the Mets this far, but it was Oliver Perez—of all peo-ple—who carried the Mets through the first six innings. Because of numer-ous injuries to starters, Perez, who equaled his Mets win total for the year with a solid start in Game 4, got the ball in Game 7. He allowed just one run but was bailed out on his final pitch by left fielder Endy Chavez, who leaped high and came down with a snow-cone catch to turn Scott Rolen's would-be home run into a double play. The Mets loaded the bases in the bottom of the inning, but NLCS MVP Jeff Suppan retired Jose Valentin and Chavez to end the threat. The game stayed tied until Yadier Molina hit a ball off Aaron Heilman that even Endy couldn't catch. Losing what turned out to be Shea Stadium's last postseason game was painful, but what hurt all the more was seeing how ripe the Tigers were for the taking in the World Series.

4. October 9, 1988: Dodgers 5, Mets 4—NLCS Game 4

Before the tragic endings of 1999 and 2006, this was the touchstone mo-ment of Mets playoff heartbreak. The 1988 NLCS turned on a home run in the ninth inning by a tough-nosed catcher with little power—sounds like 2006, huh? Dwight Gooden was on the mound at Shea Stadium in the ninth with a man on and a 4–2 lead as Randy Myers warmed in the bullpen. Yet, Doc faced Mike Scioscia and allowed the fatal longball. Ironi-cally, Scioscia was pinch-hit for later in the game when he faced the lefty Myers. Kirk Gibson hit a deciding home run off Roger McDowell in the twelfth. The Mets were tortured in the bottom of the inning, as ex-Mets Tim Leary and Jesse Orosco got outs before series MVP (and the previous day's starter) Orel Hershiser came in to get the last out with the bases full.

5. October 21, 1973: A's 5, Mets 2—World Series Game 7

After shooting from last place to first in a month to steal the division title, the Mets were playing with house money, yet when you have a three-games-to-two World Series lead, it's pretty tough to lose both games, even on the road—just ask the 1986 Red Sox. Second-guessers say that Yogi Berra should have used George Stone in Game 6 and saved a rested Seaver for Game 7, but, with a chance to win the title, it was pretty hard to pass

Best Mets on Opening Day

The Mets have the best record in major league history on Opening Day. In their first fifty openers, the Mets put together a mark of 32–18 (.640). Their record in their first fifty seasons minus the openers is 3,779–4,131 (.478). Tip of the cap to Mark Simon at ESPN.com for inspiration.

On the Mound: Tom Seaver

Seaver was 6–0 with a 2.13 ERA in eleven season openers for the Mets. (He was terrific in other games as well.) Dwight Gooden was awfully good in his eight lid lifters: 6–1 with a 3.65 ERA.

At the Plate: Darryl Strawberry

Strawberry opened the season in right field for the Mets from 1984 to 1990, the club's most prolific period of success. The Mets went 5–2 in those openers, dropping the first and the last with Straw manning right. In openers, he batted .500 in twenty-two at bats, with four home runs and eight RBI.

Leading Off: Jose Reyes

Jose led off the season in a Mets record seven-straight Opening Days (2005–2011), surpassing the mark of five set by Mookie Wilson in the 1980s. The first Met to lead off a season more than once was Tommie Agee, who opened the season for the 1969–1971 Mets. Bud Harrelson and Vince Coleman also led off the season three times apiece. Lee Mazzilli, Wally Backman, Lenny Dykstra, Lance Johnson, Rickey Henderson, and Roger Cedeno each performed the feat twice as Mets.

Debuting: Kaz Matsui

His contributions to the Mets the rest of the year were so-so (at best), but the slight infielder with the weak arm hit like Hideki Matsui in his first at bat each season. He homered as the leadoff hitter in his major league debut in 2004. He also homered in his first at bat—batting in the two hole—in 2005. He homered his first time up in 2006—an inside-the-park job to boot—but his season opened three weeks after everyone else's because of injury.

Bowing Out: Mike Howard

The Opening Day right fielder in 1983—the day Tom Seaver returned to the Mets—Mike Howard snapped a scoreless tie with a bases-loaded single in the seventh inning against Phillies ace Steve Carlton. It did not get Seaver the win, but it did provide rookie Doug Sisk his first career victory. Howard never played in the majors again after that day.

on Seaver, the Cy Young winner, for Stone, who would win exactly five more games in his career after 1973. If Stone had been pounded, people would still be complaining about that. Seaver lost Game 6, and Jon Matlack started Game 7. Matlack had been brilliant in the postseason, but, in his third start of the World Series, he surrendered two home runs in the third inning, and the A's held on for their second straight world championship.

☾ Top Ten Games, Regular Season ☾

In the postseason, you go in hoping that every game is going to be memorable, but during the regular season, any game can suddenly turn into one for the ages. It can be a must-win that they actually won or a night when what looked like a sure loss suddenly turned Amazin'. Here's a look at those days and nights when everyone wished they were at the Mets game.

1. October 3, 1999: Mets 2, Pirates 1

It's a tough call for the top spot, but name one other time the Mets actually won on the final day of the year when they needed to. (Give up? 1973, a year represented later on this list.) After an ill-timed 1–8 stretch to close out September put the 1999 Mets two games out of the Wild Card with three games remaining, they won twice against Pittsburgh while the Reds dropped two straight in Milwaukee. The Mets and Reds both needed to win their final games to force a one-game playoff. The Pirates scored early, and rookie Kris Benson was superb, but the Mets tied the game in the fourth. It was still 1–1 in the ninth when Armando Benitez fanned Aramis Ramirez with two men on. In the bottom of the inning, Melvin Mora singled, and Edgardo Alfonzo's hit sent him to third. John Olerud was walked to set up a force, and Brad Clontz was brought in to try to get Mike Piazza. The first pitch skipped to the backstop, and Mora pounced on home. Unbridled joy filled Shea Stadium, and another date was added to the calendar.

2. October 4, 1999: Mets 5, Reds 0

Game 163 is considered a regular-season game, and the Mets have had few bigger. Al Leiter, 12–12 on the year, faced 11–3 Steve Parris in Cincinnati in the first one-game playoff in either club's history. Two batters into the game the Mets had a 2–0 lead on Edgardo Alfonzo's home run. Denny Neagle walked in a run, Rickey Henderson added a home run, and Alfonzo notched another RBI. The rest was all Leiter, who took a one-hitter into the ninth before allowing a double and a walk. Alfonzo snared a liner on Leiter's 135th pitch to end the game and put the Mets in the postseason for the first time since 1988.

3. September 21, 2001: Mets 3, Braves 2

This game belongs in its own category, but it would be improper to omit the most emotional game in Mets history. In the first outdoor sporting event in New York following the September 11 tragedy, there wasn't a dry eye in the house. The fallen were remembered, and flags, fire fighters, police, and every organization that took part in the rescue were represented. The Mets, on a 19–5 run, had cut the deficit from 13½ to 5½ games behind Atlanta. The Braves took the lead in the top of the eighth against the defending league champion Mets, but Edgardo Alfonzo worked out a walk in the bottom of the inning. Long Island's Steve Karsay got ahead 0–1 and then threw one of the most memorable pitches in franchise history to Mike Piazza. Howie Rose called it on TV: "[Javy] Lopez wants it away, and it's hit deep to left center, Andruw Jones on the run, this one has a chance . . . home run!" Baseball did what it always does—it continued its daily existence. People followed.

4. September 20, 1973: Mets 4, Pirates 3

The Mets ended August in last place and began October celebrating the division title. In between came the most Amazin' win by Yogi Berra's club. With the Mets down a run and down to their last out at Shea, Duffy Dyer's double tied the game. In the top of the thirteenth, rookie Dave Augustine hit a drive that struck the narrow top of the fence, but, instead of landing in the bullpen for a home run, it caromed to Cleon Jones, who threw to Wayne Garrett, who fired to Ron Hodges, who tagged out Richie Zisk at the plate. While fans were still marveling at the "The Ball on the Wall" play, Hodges singled in the winning run in the bottom of the inning. The next night, the Mets took over first place for good.

5. July 9, 1969: Mets 4, Cubs 0

Of Tom Seaver's twenty-five wins in 1969, none was as dominating as his "Imperfect Game." At jam-packed Shea against the first-place Cubs, Tom Terrific lived up to the billing. He retired the first twenty-five batters, including Randy Hundley on a bunt attempt to start the ninth. Obscure rookie Jimmy Qualls then singled to left to break up the bid. Seaver finished with a one-hitter, and the Mets served notice that not only was Seaver the league's best pitcher but also his team was very much for real.

6. September 15, 1969: Mets 4, Cardinals 3

In a season in which every ball seemed to bounce the right way, black cats spooked the opposition, pitchers knocked in runs when the offense disappeared, and the *other* team lost flyballs in the sun for a change, Ron Swoboda ruined Steve Carlton's one-man show in St. Louis. Carlton became the first pitcher in history with nineteen strikeouts in a nine-inning game—and the first to fan nineteen and lose. Swoboda was twice a victim and twice a slugger, collecting a pair of two-run homers to push the first-place Mets to victory over the Cards and increase their lead to 4½ games.

7. September 24, 1969: Mets 6, Cardinals 0

Rarely has wanton destruction of public property felt so right. After striking out nineteen Mets his last time facing them, Steve Carlton didn't make it out of the first inning. Donn Clendenon homered twice, and Ed Charles laced his last career home run. Gary Gentry put a bow on the shutout and division clincher by inducing Joe Torre to bounce into a double play at 9:07 p.m., setting off a wild celebration in the stands, on the field, and in the locker room at Shea Stadium. "A scene of wild jubilation," as announcer Lindsey Nelson described it. And, as if everything wasn't working perfectly for the 1969 Mets, since this was the season's final home game, groundskeeper Pete Flynn had eleven days to get the field back in order . . . so it could be torn up again.

8. April 22, 1970: Mets 2, Padres 1

On a Wednesday afternoon before 14,197 at Shea, Tom Seaver tied Steve Carlton's record of nineteen strikeouts the hard way—by setting a new mark and striking out the last ten batters he faced. Al Ferrera homered off Seaver in the second inning and then started the conga line of K's in the sixth. Nate Colbert, Dave Campbell, and Jerry Morales went down in the seventh; Bob Barton, Ramon Webster, and Ivan Murrell followed suit in the eighth; and Van Kelly, Cito Gaston, and Ferrera fanned in the ninth. Seaver had been given his 1969 Cy Young earlier in the day—it would not be his last.

9. July 10, 1999: Mets 9, Yankees 8

For the first time, both the Mets and Yankees hosted games against each other. This seesaw game, the fifth between the clubs in 1999, saw the Yankees leading by a run at Shea with Mariano Rivera in to close it out. But Bernie Williams let a flyball fall in for a double, and, after retiring John Olerud, Rivera walked Mike Piazza, who'd hit a titanic home run earlier. Matt Franco batted for Melvin Mora with two outs. The Yankees, who'd clubbed six home runs in the game, had won 124 straight games in which they led in the ninth. Franco had other plans, singling home the tying and winning runs. This dramatic win—in a year where every win was needed—

displaced Dave Mlicki's 1997 inaugural interleague shutout as the brightest moment in Mets subway-series history.

10. June 14, 1980: Mets 7, Giants 6

This game is a tribute to the fans who stuck with the Mets during seven straight years of fifth place or lower. After finishing last three straight years, the Mets were two games under .500 and six games out the night before Father's Day. The Giants were shelling them, but the shelling stopped after San Francisco went up 6–0 in the fifth. The Mets managed single runs in the sixth and eighth, but they were down to their last out when Lee Mazzilli's hit brought in Doug Flynn in the ninth. Frank Taveras walked, Claudell Washington singled, and starter Allen Ripley came out of the bullpen to pitch to Steve Henderson, a cleanup hitter without a home run. After ducking away from a pitch near his chin, Hendu slammed a drive to right that landed in the bullpen for a stunning comeback win. For a limited time only, the magic was back.

☻ Most Heartbreaking Mets Losses, Regular Season ☻

These may have been even more devastating than were the crushing losses of the postseason. At least those involved winning something before losing. **Warning:** Spending too much time on these moments may result in costly psychoanalysis or an exorbitant bar bill.

1. September 30, 2007: Marlins 8, Mets 1

Seven-game lead . . . seventeen games left . . . Phillies gaining . . . Nationals whipping . . . Wagner's back ailing . . . Marlins out for blood . . . can't write in complete sentences . . . thank you, Maine . . . tied, one game left . . . no, Glavine, no—put down the ball . . . 7–0 in the first . . . auuugghhhh!!!!!

2. September 28, 2008: Marlins 4, Mets 2

Same win-or-die scenario, same teams playing in the last game, same location, but 2008 had more drama and more hope, even with Oliver Perez on the mound. Ollie kept the Mets in the game, Endy Chavez made

Best Mets Comebacks

What many consider the greatest Mets moment was a comeback. They came back from two runs down with two men out in Game 6 of the 1986 World Series. The Mets were three runs down in the deciding World Series games in both 1969 and 1986, and they won both times. The same thing happened in the 1986 NLCS clincher. In Game 3 of the 1986 NLCS, they had been down by four before winning. In short, comebacks aren't new for New York's underdog club.

During the regular season, the Mets have come back from even larger deficits. Fifteen times, they have rebounded from six runs down to win. Far rarer have been comebacks from seven runs down or more, including putting up a late touchdown to win in 2011.

Eight Runs Down: Mets 11, Astros 8 (September 2, 1972)

The previous night, the Mets had lost in Houston by an 8–0 score, with Tom Seaver on the mound. Down 8–0 again and facing Astros ace Don Wilson with only two innings remaining in the game, the comeback started with a Duffy Dyer single. Another single, a walk, a sacrifice fly, and a three-run home run by Ken Boswell chased Wilson and made it 8–4. The Mets wound up scoring seven and stranding the tying run at second. The tying run scored on an error in the ninth, and Cleon Jones and Wayne Garrett each had their second run-scoring hit in as many innings as the Mets came all the way back.

Seven Runs Down: Mets 9, Pirates 8 (June 2, 2011)

It seems like only yesterday. . . . Down 7–0 in the bottom of the third inning, Jose Reyes and Justin Turner singled with two out and none on. Carlos Beltran crushed a three-run homer, and it was a ballgame again. Beltran doubled in the sixth and Jason Bay walked, but it looked like Pirate Paul Maholm would escape. But Ruben Tejada's opposite-field, two-run single and a Daniel Murphy run-scoring pinch hit was followed by a passed ball to make it 7–7. After sending up a pitcher to bunt in a tie game in the eighth, a balk made Manager Terry Collins rethink the strategy, and Josh Thole came out to bat with a 1–1 count. Four walks later, the Mets had the lead. Francisco Rodriguez survived the ninth, and the Mets had quite the weekday matinee win.

Seven Runs Down: Mets 11, Braves 8 (June 30, 2000)

With the Mets down 8–1 in the eighth inning, most of the crowd of 52,831 had stuck around Shea only to see the postgame fireworks. The second out of the home eighth brought in a run for an 8–2 score. Todd Zeile and Jay Payton followed with singles, and Kerry Ligtenberg was summoned, beginning a merry-go-round of four straight walks that made it 8–6. Edgardo Alfonzo lined a single that plated two and tied the game. Mike Piazza followed with an exclamation point that clunked off the façade in left field for a three-run blast. The Mets had a seven-run comeback and a ten-run inning. Now that's fireworks.

a homer-saving catch, and Carlos Beltran hit the final Mets home run at Shea Stadium to tie the game in the sixth inning. Unfortunately, that was upstaged by consecutive blasts by Wes Helms and Dan Uggla in the eighth. Ryan Church made the final out in Shea Stadium history, and the Brewers took the Wild Card. At least there was a nice ceremony to commemorate Shea after the game.

3. June 12, 2009: Yankees 9, Mets 8

Luis Castillo's dropped pop-up with two outs in the ninth not only allowed the tying and winning runs to score, it also ended Francisco Rodriguez's run of fourteen straight saves to begin his Mets career, handed the second-place Mets a soul-crushing defeat in their first-ever game at the new Yankee Stadium, and signaled that the Mets' mojo was still busted.

Drop and Give Me Twenty: Marathons

Through 2011, the Dodgers appeared in the most twenty-inning games in history, but the Mets had the market cornered on quantity in terms of innings. No other team has seen the twenty-third inning or later more often than the bleary-eyed Mets—or their fans. The Mets have played games lasting twenty-three, twenty-four, and twenty-five innings—and lost them all. On their fourth try past the twenty-inning barrier, the Mets finally won.

April 17, 2010: Mets 2, Cardinals 1

Facing their second infielder/pitcher of the day/night in St. Louis, Jose Reyes knocked in the go-ahead run in the top of the twentieth against Joe Mather. Mather, who'd played center field and third base earlier in the game, was making his first competitive pitching appearance since his sophomore year in high school. Mike Pelfrey, who'd thrown seven shutout innings two days earlier, tossed another scoreless frame for the save. Francisco Rodriguez got the win despite blowing a save an inning earlier. The Mets used everyone on the roster except the previous night's starter, Oliver Perez.
Duration: 6 hours, 53 minutes

September 11, 1974: Cardinals 4, Mets 3

A generation earlier, the Mets and Cardinals locked horns for twenty-five innings in the longest game played to a conclusion in National League history. (A twenty-six-inning tie game between Brooklyn and Boston was called by darkness in 1920.) The twenty-five-inning game at Shea saw the Mets lose when Bake McBride scored from first on a wild pickoff throw by Hank Webb.
Duration: 7 hours, 4 minutes

April 15, 1968: Astros 1, Mets 0

This was the longest Mets road game ever. There was no happy recap at the Astrodome. In just the fifth game of Gil Hodges's Mets managing career, shortstop Al Weis's error let the game's only run score. General Manager Johnny Murphy insisted the error happened because the dirt infield hadn't been worked on for hours. He successfully petitioned to have fields dragged every seven innings, no matter how long the game went.

Duration: 6 hours, 6 minutes

May 31, 1964: Giants 8, Mets 6

It wasn't just another doubleheader loss in Shea Stadium's inaugural year. The nightcap featured a Mets triple play in extra innings and Gaylord Perry perfecting his spitball during a ten-inning relief stretch for San Francisco. Umpire Ed Sudol saw every pitch—as he would for the twenty-four- and twenty-five-inning games the Mets played over the next decade.

Duration: 7 hours, 23 minutes

4. April 26, 1995: Rockies 11, Mets 9

This first game following the cataclysmic 1994 strike was . . . well, so damned annoying. It also served as a public-service alert to the National League for those wearing road grays at brand-new Coors Field. The Mets, who actually fell behind, 5–1, blew leads in the ninth, thirteenth, and fourteenth innings. Dante Bichette's three-run walkoff homer off Mike Remlinger became an inspirational video at the ballpark for years to come.

5. October 3, 1985: Cardinals 4, Mets 3

Unlike the other losses on this list, you could be proud of this game. The Mets had stayed with the Cardinals all year, had given the Cards everything they had, and had beaten St. Louis in the first two games of this must-win series at Busch Stadium. But this loss still stung. Keith Hernandez had five hits yet did not score. Rookies Rick Aguilera and Roger McDowell pitched well on the big stage but for naught. The loss all but eliminated the Mets, who stood two games out with three to play. There was no miracle in 1985, but a resolve was forged to finish second to no one in 1986.

Mets People

Eddie Boison: "Cowbell Man"

Cowbell Man is easy to hear but hard to track down at Citi Field. Harder still is deciding how to write "Let's Go Mets" in his language: "DONK! DONK! DONK!"

But the first question is the simplest: why the cowbell? "I used to play in a Latin band and I brought a cowbell to a game at Shea to do some practice back in 1995," says Eddie Boison, aka Cowbell Man. "Diamond Vision put up 'Let's Go Mets,' and I started playing along with their rendition. Then people started to applaud. I brought the cowbell back to another game and saw that people were responding."

"I've got a fever and the only prescription is more cowbell!"
—*Christopher Walken on* Saturday Night Live

That 1995 season was shortened by eighteen games due to the lingering strike that had canceled the 1994 World Series. Shea was dead and the team was far from great. What could one man do to help? To quote Christopher Walken on *Saturday Night Live* in the most famous cowbell skit ever: "I've got a fever and the only prescription is more cowbell!"

Boison, who works in the hospital food-services industry, has been prescribing the cowbell cure to Mets fans in increasingly large doses. It began with a Tuesday-Friday ticket plan and progressed to a season ticket. Now he only misses a game in case of a family emergency. He pays his own way at Citi Field, like any fan. Cowbell Man knows his history when it comes to baseball's great cowbell moments: Hilda Chester at Ebbets Field, the many cowbell enthusiasts at Yankee Stadium, and the Tampa Bay Rays adopting the instrument during their run to the 2008 American League pennant.

But there's a right way to play it. Cowbell Man will let anyone hit it, even though that leads to it being struck too hard and eventually breaking. He goes through a new instrument—he buys them for $50–$60 apiece—about every three years. He does offer a tip to future cowbell strikers: "Hit it right in the middle. People think you have to hit it hard. Just tap it and the sound takes care of itself."

He was born in 1957, the year the Dodgers and Giants moved to California. Boison has spent his whole life in, of all places, the Bronx. His father, a native of Puerto Rico, was a National League fan and took his son to his first Mets game the first month Shea Stadium opened in 1964. Boison took notice of Shea's most conspicuous and famous fan: "The Sign Man," Karl Ehrhardt. "The best one was just two letters, one sign said 'A' and the other 'G' for Tommie Agee. He'd hold them up and people used to cheer that," he says. "When they beat the Orioles in the World Series, he had a great sign: 'Bye Bye Birdies.'"

Cowbell Man is friendly with all the newer sign men at Citi Field and is friendly with everyone, for that matter. How could someone who spends every game moving from section to section, making noise and creating smiles at every stop, not be friendly? (Though he will vacate an area if someone—who apparently has forgotten they are *at a ballgame*—complains about noise.) Shea Stadium was a better venue for his musical craft because he could spend several innings at a time going from the end of one deck to the other. Citi Field requires going up a lot more stairs, plus much more concourse crossing, resulting in Cowbell Man being heard more than he's seen. But, maybe, that is his Citi Field legacy. Go to a game, and you're bound to hear him and probably cheer him. "DONK! DONK! DONK!"

CHAPTER

4

The All-Star Break

UST LIKE THE ALL-STAR GAME, which comes a little more than halfway through the season, here is a brief respite a little past the book's midway point to discuss Mets All-Star performances. Don't worry; it won't take long.

The Mets came into being during the last year that two All-Star Games were played. (Two All-Star Games were played from 1959 to 1962 to help build up the major league player pension fund.) Mets center fielder Richie Ashburn was named a reserve for both All-Star Games in 1962 despite the fact that his team was thirty-six games under .500 for the July 10 affair in Washington and fifty games under for the July 30 matinee at Wrigley Field—the Mets squeezed in an eleven-game losing streak between Midsummer Classics. Ashburn sat out the National League's win in D.C., but he singled and scored in his only at bat in the All-Star Game at Wrigley. Per usual that year, Ashburn's positive contribution went for naught in a blowout loss.

☙ Best Mets All-Star Starters ☙

Through the years, there have been Mets that have deserved to be All-Stars and did not make it because of a numbers crunch. And there have been Mets who were named because every team is required to have an All-Star. Starters have come in bunches: thirteen in a six-year span in the 1980s

Table 4.1. Mets Starters, All-Star Game

Year	Mets Starter	Position
1964	Ron Hunt	2B
1968	Jerry Grote	C
1969	Cleon Jones	LF
1970	Tom Seaver	P
1971	Bud Harrelson	SS
1972	Willie Mays	CF
1976	Dave Kingman	RF
1984	Darryl Strawberry	RF
1985	Darryl Strawberry	RF
	Gary Carter[a]	C
1986	Dwight Gooden	P
	Gary Carter	C
	Keith Hernandez	1B
	Darryl Strawberry	RF
1987	Gary Carter	C
	Darryl Strawberry	RF
1988	Gary Carter	C
	Darryl Strawberry	RF
1989	Howard Johnson[b]	3B
	Darryl Strawberry[a]	RF
1996	Lance Johnson[b]	CF
1998	Mike Piazza	C
1999	Mike Piazza	C
2000	Mike Piazza[a]	C
2001	Mike Piazza	C
2002	Mike Piazza	C
2004	Mike Piazza	C
2005	Mike Piazza	C
	Carlos Beltran	CF
2006	Paul LoDuca	C
	David Wright	3B
	Carlos Beltran	CF
	Jose Reyes[a]	SS
2007	Jose Reyes	SS
	David Wright	3B
	Carlos Beltran	CF
2009	David Wright	3B
2010	David Wright	3B
2011	Carlos Beltran	DH

[a] Indicates player was chosen to start but could not play due to injury.

[b] Indicates player started in place of another player.

after none were elected for eight years prior to that. Mets at every position have started the All-Star Game, with Mike Piazza's seven starts the standard.

☙ Truly All-Star Performances ☙

Only Jon Matlack, the winner of the 1975 All-Star Game, has taken the game's MVP Award back to Flushing. And, with Matlack sharing the prize with Bill Madlock of the Cubs, you almost get the idea that someone should have called for a recount to make sure everyone got the right spelling on the ballots. But give Big Jon his due as well as the other Mets who have made their Midsummer Classic dreams come true for a night.

Lee Mazzilli, 1979

Maz hit the game-tying home run batting left-handed off Jim Kern and drew a tiebreaking bases-loaded walk in the ninth against Yankee Ron Guidry at the Kingdome. Pirates right fielder Dave Parker got the MVP, the only time the award has been doled out for a great throw.

Lance Johnson, 1996

In the midst of the year of his life, Lance had the night of his life at Veterans Stadium. Starting in center field in place of injured Tony Gwynn, Johnson batted leadoff and went three for four with a double and a stolen base while playing the entire game. It was his only All-Star appearance and the National League's only win for fifteen years.

Tom Seaver, 1970

In a dream matchup between Seaver and Baltimore's Jim Palmer nine months after the Mets stunned the Orioles in the World Series, both pitchers allowed just one hit in three scoreless innings. In the longest stint by a Met in an All-Star Game, Seaver fanned four—three of whom he would later join in Cooperstown. Remarkably, this was Tom Terrific's only All-Star start in a dozen trips to the Midsummer Classic. Seaver didn't get the win in Cincinnati, but Manager Gil Hodges did.

Dwight Gooden, 1984

Rookie Doc Gooden's three strikeouts in the fifth inning weren't against Hall of Famers, but coming an inning after Fernando Valenzuela fanned the side—future Cooperstown inductees all—Gooden's troika broke Carl Hubbell's 1934 mark, with six straight strikeouts by one league. Doc got Lance Parrish, Chet Lemon, and Al Davis swinging at air. He tossed a scoreless sixth as well in San Francisco in the NL's 3–1 win.

Carlos Beltran, 2006; Jose Reyes, 2007

Call this a tie—no, wait, that would be the 2002 All-Star Game. Anyway, Beltran was in the running for MVP in 2006, going two for four with a daring steal of third to set up his scoring the tiebreaking run on a wild pitch. (The NL's other run came on a David Wright home run.) Beltran played the whole game, which meant he watched as Michael Young's two-out, two-run triple in the ninth off Trevor Hoffman brought in the tying and winning runs in Pittsburgh. Jose Reyes missed that game with a hand injury, but he was fired up in 2007, going three for four with a double, a run, and a stolen base in the 5–4 loss in San Francisco.

⚾ All-Star Managers, Recaps ⚾

A fringe benefit of going to a World Series is getting to manage the All-Star Game the following year. Mets managers have earned the honor four times, with four different men guiding the National League's best players for a game. The quartet has won three of four times.

Gil Hodges, 1970

The most memorable game of the four began with Tom Seaver tossing three superb innings as the National League starter. The NL trailed 4–1 heading into the ninth. Bud Harrelson, who singled twice, came around to score for the second time, and Joe Morgan later scored to tie the game. The game was still tied in the twelfth at brand-new Riverfront Stadium when Jim Hickman singled with two men on. The throw beat Pete Rose, but he barreled over catcher Ray Fosse to secure the NL's eighth victory in a row. Don't tell Charlie Hustle it's a meaningless exhibition.

Yogi Berra, 1974

It was the first All-Star Game of Tom Seaver's eight-year career that he was not invited to, due to injury and a 6–6 record, but Jon Matlack (9–6, 2.59 ERA) did qualify for Yogi's squad and tossed a scoreless inning. Pirate Ken Brett picked up the win in Pittsburgh, and iron Dodger Mike Marshall, as he would do a record 106 times, came out of the pen to subdue the opposition. It looked like the manager in the other dugout would be Baltimore's Earl Weaver, but Dick Williams got back his rightful spot. Williams had quit the A's minutes after his team vanquished the Mets in the 1973 World Series; the Angels hired Williams on July 1, 1974.

Davey Johnson, 1987

In a year of marked offense, the All-Star Game had none. The game was scoreless for twelve innings before the game's MVP Tim Raines mercifully tripled home two runs. Davey Johnson, who brought four Mets with him to Oakland, kept Sid Fernandez in reserve to pitch the thirteenth. He joined starters Tom Seaver (1967) and Jerry Koosman (1968) as Mets pitchers with All-Star saves.

Bobby Valentine, 2000

Baseball fans across the country remember this game for Texas shortstop Alex Rodriguez moving to third base so that Baltimore's Cal Ripken, playing the final season of his illustrious career, could start one last time at the position he dominated. New Yorkers remember the All-Star Game in Seattle for the Mike Piazza–Roger Clemens grudge match that resulted in seven pitches nowhere close to Piazza and a flyout to right. Ripken homered to earn MVP as Bobby V.'s side fell to Joe Torre's, 4–1. Again.

◌ The All-Star Shaft ◌

A poorly-kept secret has the Mets hosting the 2013 All-Star Game. It's about time. No team in history has waited as long as the New York Mets between All-Star Game hosting assignments. Every team except the Florida Marlins and Tampa Bay Rays, who entered the majors in the 1990s, has

1964: Best—and Only—Mets All-Star Game

The Mets hosted just one All-Star Game in their first fifty years, but it sure was a doozy.

Shea Stadium was brand-spanking new under the July sunshine—yes, it was so long ago the game was still played in the afternoon—and the Mets employed their first All-Star starter. Lovable Ron Hunt was selected to start—and not in some popularity contest because Mets fans stuffed the ballot boxes. Fans in Cincinnati had been guilty of doing so in 1957—the public didn't get the vote back until 1970—so the 1964 All-Stars were chosen by ballot from 270 players, coaches, and managers. Hunt, batting .322 when the votes were announced, had three times more votes at second base than Pittsburgh's Bill Mazeroski, the 1960 World Series hero and future Hall of Famer.

The twenty-three-year-old Hunt had a good day, though the National League did not—until the ninth inning. Hunt, who went one for three, was pinch-hit for with two on and one out in the ninth by Hank Aaron. The NL had just tied the game on an error, but Aaron missed a chance to be a hero when he struck out. Up stepped Philadelphia's Johnny Callison, who launched an opposite-field home run to right field, off Boston's Dick Radatz, to win the game and claim the MVP. Juan Marichal got the win. Ken Boyer and Billy Williams also hit homers for the NL as the stars aligned for a day at Shea.

hosted at least one All-Star Game since the Mets last served as host in 1964, the year Shea Stadium opened.

Some sources claim the Mets were not interested in hosting the event in the 1980s and that Major League Baseball insisted the team first replace Shea Stadium before resuming host duties. The assignments for the All-Star Game since the Mets came into existence in 1962 are listed below.

Note: Two All-Star Games were played in 1962. The Kansas City Royals are to be 2012 hosts, and the Washington Senators and Texas Rangers (Arlington) are listed separately.

Three Times as All-Star Hosts

Cleveland: 1963, 1981 (Municipal Stadium); 1997 (Jacobs Field)
Anaheim: 1967, 1989, 2010
Houston: 1968, 1986 (Astrodome); 2004 (Minute Maid Park)
Pittsburgh: 1974, 1994 (Three Rivers Stadium); 2006 (PNC Park)

Twice as All-Star Hosts

Washington Senators: 1962, 1969
Chicago Cubs: 1962, 1989
Minneapolis: 1965 (Metropolitan Stadium); 1985 (Metrodome)
St. Louis: 1966 (Busch Stadium II); 2008 (Busch III)
Cincinnati: 1970, 1988
Detroit: 1971 (Tiger Stadium); 2005 (Comerica Park)
Atlanta: 1972 (Fulton County Stadium); 2000 (Turner Field)
Milwaukee: 1975 (County Stadium); 2002 (Miller Park)
Philadelphia: 1976, 1996
New York Yankees: 1977, 2008
San Diego: 1978, 1992
Seattle: 1979 (Kingdome); 2001 (Safeco Park)
Chicago White Sox: 1983 (Comiskey Park); 2003 (U.S. Cellular Field)
San Francisco: 1984 (Candlestick Park); 2007 (AT&T Park)

Once as All-Star Hosts

New York Mets: 1964
Kansas City: 1973
Los Angeles Dodgers: 1980
Montreal: 1982
Oakland: 1987
Toronto: 1991
Baltimore: 1993
Arlington: 1995
Denver: 1998
Boston: 1999
Phoenix: 2011

Best Mets Who Call the Shots

⚬ Best Mets Managers ⚬

DON'T YOU JUST HATE IT when someone throws together a list of great players but leaves out the managers? So do I. Someone has to make out the lineup and make up things to say to keep the press happy. The Mets have had managers who weren't so hot, but these five skippers are as good as it gets.

1. Gil Hodges (1968–1971)

If you win a World Series with a team that had undoubtedly been the worst team in baseball for the past seven years, you get the top spot. This ranking was seconded at a Mets Booster Club meeting at SpringHill Suites in Port St. Lucie in March 2011 by none other than Ron Darling. The 1986 veteran and respected announcer acknowledged "the '69 Mets *are* the Mets" and praised the managing effort of Gil in 1969 as one of the greatest in history. All in favor? Aye.

2. Davey Johnson (1984–1990)

Whereas Gil Hodges quietly encouraged a team of young ballplayers to play to their full potential, Davey Johnson—who, ironically, made the last out of the 1969 World Series as an Oriole—let his guys play and reined them in as needed (and, famously, paid the tab for the interior of a plane they destroyed after winning the 1986 pennant). The 1984–1990 Mets should have produced another World Series, but be thankful for small miracles and a franchise record .588 winning percentage under Davey Johnson.

3. Bobby Valentine (1996–2002)

Like Davey Johnson, he had great success but was fired after one bad season. When Valentine came to Flushing in 1996, the Mets were a disappointing mess, and no one thought much of their chances. His club won eighteen more games in 1997, and he kept the team in the headlines despite the fact that the Yankees were at their peak of the last half century. He is the only Mets manager to take the team to the postseason two straight years—losing to said Yankees in the 2000 World Series—and it was a sad day for the Mets when they fired Bobby V. Many still want to see him back.

"When you come to a fork in the road, take it."—Yogi Berra

4. Yogi Berra (1972–1975)

"It ain't over 'til it's over"—Yogi came up with the line during the summer of 1973 as manager of the Mets. As usual, his folksy wisdom showed prescience and insight. It wasn't over. The Mets went from last to first in the final month of 1973, beat the Big Red Machine in the NLCS, and wound up one win shy of a world championship against the Swingin' A's. Some still blame Yogi for pitching Tom Seaver on short rest instead of George Stone, when the Mets needed to win only one of the last two in Oakland (they won neither). To that, quoth Yogi: "When you come to a fork in the road, take it."

5. Willie Randolph (2005–2008)

He's no Gil, Davey, Bobby, or even Yogi, but Willie brought life to a dead team when he took over in 2005 (it didn't hurt that Pedro Martinez and Carlos Beltran arrived in Flushing with him). His 2006 team spent just one day all season out of first place, and with the starting staff decimated before the Division Series, Randolph used every arm at his disposal, often

Table 5.1.   Mets Manager Roll Call

Manager	Seasons	Record
Casey Stengel	3½	175–404
Wes Westrum	2½	142–237
Salty Parker	1967 Interim	4–7
Gil Hodges	4	339–309
Yogi Berra	3⅔	292–296
Roy McMillan	1975 Interim	26–27
Joe Frazier	1⅓	101–106
Joe Torre	4⅔	286–420
George Bamberger	1⅓	81–127
Frank Howard	1983 Interim	52–64
Davey Johnson	6⅓	595–417
Bud Harrelson	1⅔	145–129
Mike Cubbage	1991 Interim	3–4
Jeff Torborg	1⅓	85–115
Dallas Green	4	229–283
Bobby Valentine	6¼	536–547
Art Howe	2	137–186
Willie Randolph	3½	302–253
Jerry Manuel	2½	204–213
Terry Collins	2011–	77–85

with good results. St. Louis had better pitching and beat the favored Mets in seven games to reach the World Series. Willie's overreliance on the pen resulted in the great collapse of 2007, and he had lost many of the fans—and some of the team—by the time of his controversial firing in June of 2008.

⚾ Best Mets General Managers ⚾

In a half century of Mets baseball, there have only been a dozen general managers. Most have been so-so. Unlike managers, who can be judged on their won-lost records, GMs are evaluated by constantly changing criteria that often take time to evaluate because deals that may be considered masterstrokes when they are made, sometimes turn into blunders a decade later. The GM is also held accountable for the players produced from the minor leagues.

1. Frank Cashen (1980–1991)

Cashen is the gold standard when it comes to Mets GMs. He took over a putrefying team and made it into a world champion in six years. And then he tore the club down by trading "undesirable" personalities and replacing them with players who proved to be bland both on and off the field. Cashen was truly deserving of induction into the Mets Hall of Fame.

Best Deals: Trading for Keith Hernandez, Gary Carter, David Cone, Sid Fernandez, Ron Darling, Bob Ojeda . . .

2. Johnny Murphy (1968–1969)

After Cashen, everybody else is a step below. Murphy was with the Mets system in 1961 and worked his way up. He arranged the deal to bring Gil Hodges to manage, shortly before Murphy was even GM. With the Mets needing a veteran in the lineup in 1969, he landed Donn Clendenon, who went on to be World Series MVP. His worst deal was trading Amos Otis and Bob Johnson to the Royals for Joe Foy weeks before Murphy's untimely death in January 1970. He was inducted into the Mets Hall of Fame in 1983.

Best Deals: Arranging for the return of Gil Hodges; drafting Rule 5 pick Wayne Garrett; trading for Donn Clendenon.

3. George Weiss (1962–1966)

Weiss gets the blame for picking the personnel that lost one-hundred-plus games for four years out of the gate, but he also hired many of the people who would have a major role in turning the team around at the end of the decade. That included two future GMs, the aforementioned Johnny Murphy and Bing Devine, who set a record for most players used in a season in 1967 and laid the groundwork for the club's rise despite only officially being GM for that one year. Weiss, former Yankees GM, is in the Halls of Fame in Cooperstown and Flushing.

Best Deals: Signed Ed Kranepool, Cleon Jones, Ron Swoboda, Tug McGraw, Jerry Koosman; drafted Nolan Ryan; approved the Mets' taking part in Tom Seaver lottery.

4. Joe McIlvaine (1993–1997)

Right-hand man under Frank Cashen, McIlvaine grew impatient of waiting for his turn and went to San Diego, where he soon realized the Padres were dismantling. He returned to New York and took over a Mets team in total disarray. He helped build up the club frugally and got decent returns on deadweight. He hired Bobby Valentine to replace Dallas Green in August 1996. McIlvaine's mistakes include overhyping "Generation K" and trading Jeff Kent for Carlos Baerga. Smooth-talking Steve Phillips took over as GM in mid-1997 partly because Joe Mac refused to have a cell phone glued to his ear.

Best Deals: Trading for John Olerud, Rico Brogna, Jose Vizcaino, and Armando Reynoso; signing Rick Reed, Lance Johnson, and Todd Pratt.

5. Steve Phillips (1997–2003)

The Frank Cashen regime drafted Phillips in 1981 and hired him for the front office in 1990. Appointed GM in July 1997, Phillips was cautious at first but helped transform the Mets from 1998 to 2000. He then became obsessed with acquiring veteran relievers while stripping the farm system—young Mets under his watch who were traded for peanuts and blossomed with other teams included Jason Isringhausen, Melvin Mora,

Table 5.2. Mets General Manager Roll Call

General Manager	Seasons	Best Finish
George Weiss	5	Ninth (1966)
Bing Devine	1	Tenth (1967)
Johnny Murphy	2	First (1969)
Bob Scheffing	5	First (1973)
Joe McDonald	5	Third (1975–1976)
Frank Cashen	12	First (1986, 1988)
Al Harazin	1½	Fifth (1992)
Joe McIlvaine	4	Second (1995)
Steve Phillips	6	Wild Card (1999–2000)
Jim Duquette	1½	Fourth (2004)
Omar Minaya	6	First (2006)
Sandy Alderson	2011–	Fourth (2011)

Cashen In

When Frank Cashen was hired to be Mets general manager shortly before spring training in 1980, the cupboard was bare. The Mets had not been competitive even before they traded Tom Seaver, and fan interest had dissipated since the day of the infamous deal on June 15, 1977. The "Midnight Massacre" darkened everything that came after it.

The first thing Cashen did was . . . nothing. The Mets made no splashy moves in his first year on the job, though Cashen did use the first pick in the draft to take a high school slugger named Darryl Strawberry. After the Mets hit a franchise-low sixty-one home runs in 1980, Cashen beefed up the offense by bringing back Rusty Staub and Dave Kingman—Kingman had also been banished in the Midnight Massacre, the same night the Mets received Steve Henderson, whom Cashen now shipped to the Cubs for Kong. Some of the moves were band-aids and crowd pleasers, and Cashen regrettably let a couple of future stars slip away in Jeff Reardon and Mike Scott. Randy Jones, the washed-up former Cy Young winner, went 1–8 his first year as a Met but did rally to go 7–10 in 1982 and end his career with exactly one hundred wins. The 1982 Mets were lucky to avoid one hundred losses, a slap in the face following Cashen's foray into the pricey world of superstars.

George Foster, a former MVP and one of the National League's most consistent sluggers with Cincinnati, had been acquired in a trade and lavished with the then-staggering sum of $2 million per year. Getting Tom Seaver back the next year from the Reds was much cheaper and much better for the Mets fans' soul. That soul was scarred when Cashen made a gross miscalculation and lost Seaver again in a free-agent compensation snafu. In the end, that left an opening in the rotation for the talented Mets rookies who were finally up from the farm. Dwight Gooden, Ron Darling, and Sid Fernandez all joined the 1984 rotation, while Cashen released several players at the end of the line that had broken camp with new manager Davey Johnson. Still, the Mets needed veteran leadership and dependability, so Cashen traded for Cincinnati starter Bruce Berenyi in June and Astros third baseman Ray Knight in August. Keith Hernandez, who came to New York in Cashen's masterstroke of June 1983, was runner-up in the NL MVP voting. The Mets went from ninety-four losses to ninety wins in one season.

Cashen boldly upped the ante, trading four young players, including crowd favorite Hubie Brooks, to the Expos for the NL's best catcher, Gary Carter, to help corral the strong young staff. The Mets won ninety-eight games and fell short the final week of the season, so Cashen again dipped into his rich minor league system to bring back southpaw Bobby Ojeda from the Red Sox and second baseman Tim Teufel from the Twins. Cashen also shipped starter Walt Terrell, who had come to New York with Darling in a 1982 steal, for a young Tigers third baseman named Howard Johnson. With the Mets out to a huge lead in 1986, Cashen showed he wasn't afraid to cast aside players that no longer fit the club, no matter how much they were owed. Foster was released in August, and Lee Mazzilli was picked up after being released by the last-place Pirates. Maz, who, like Mookie Wilson and Jesse Orosco, had preceded Cashen's arrival in New York, came through with several key hits during the magical October run that ended with a world championship. Calvin Schiraldi, a former Cashen number-one draft pick who'd been traded the previous winter for Ojeda, suffered the losses for Boston in Games 6 and 7.

Winning two world championships was a feat that no team managed in the 1980s—except for the Dodgers. Right-hander David Cone, swindled from the Royals just before the 1987 season started, went 20–3 and finished third in the Cy Young voting in his second full major league season in 1988. Kevin McReynolds, acquired from San Diego in a multiplayer deal that cost the Mets Kevin Mitchell, was superb in 1987 and 1988, finishing third the latter year in the MVP voting (Darryl Strawberry finished second to Dodger Kirk Gibson). The Mets pulled away to win the division crown and claim one hundred wins for the second time in three years, but they were stunned in the NLCS in seven games by Los Angeles. Cashen tried to change the culture in the locker room, but this remaking of the Mets did not take.

Cashen traded many of the players who had come up through the system, swapping out the top of the order in Lenny Dykstra and Wally Backman, the back of the bullpen in Roger McDowell and Rick Aguilera, the veteran depth in Mookie Wilson and Lee Mazzilli, and the team cocaptains, Keith Hernandez and Gary Carter, whose contracts were not renewed after the 1989 season. Strawberry, likewise, was allowed to leave. The concept of replacing him with Vince Coleman was absurd.

Sending five pitchers to the Twins for former Cy Young winner Frank Viola in 1989 got the Mets a twenty-game winner in 1990, but a month after Viola pitched his last game for the Mets in 1991, the Twins won the World Series with significant contributions from ex-Mets Kevin Tapani and Aguilera. By the end of that season, Cashen's time at the top had come to a close as well. The Mets finished fifth, just as they had his first year. Cashen retired and let the front office he'd put together run the show. The Mets would not be the same again.

and Jason Bay. In 2002, he brought in the bloated contracts of Mo Vaughn, Roger Cedeno, and David Weathers, plus the shell of once-great Roberto Alomar. He got approval to fire nemesis Bobby Valentine, stayed on as GM, and hired Art Howe. Phillips was canned the following June with the Mets in last place.

Best Deals: Acquired Al Leiter, Dennis Cook, and Mike Piazza (in three deals with Marlins); acquired Armando Benitez and Roger Cedeno (when they were good); drafted David Wright and signed Jose Reyes (and didn't trade either).

⚾ Best Trades ⚾

If people like to argue about baseball, something they really enjoy arguing about is the best trades their favorite team has made. It's a "can't lose" argument. And while the majority of the worst Mets trades occurred before 1978, all of the best trades—at least this grouping—occurred from 1983 forward. Frank Cashen pulled off three of these deals on the way to building a championship club.

1. Keith Hernandez (June 15, 1983)

This is where it all began. The Cardinals' impatience with the Gold Glove former batting champ and MVP was the first step in transforming the Mets from perennial also-ran into consistent contender. Hernandez solidified the infield as well as the entire team. You can thank Rusty Staub for schooling Mex on the benefits of living in New York. Hernandez provided experience and advice for all the young players that came up in the months and years after he came over for the puny price of Neil Allen and Rick Ownbey. The Mets even named Mex the first captain in team history.

2. Mike Piazza (May 22, 1998)

Like the Keith Hernandez deal fifteen years earlier, a superstar arrived on a platter thanks to a former team's dissatisfaction with its superstar. The price was future All-Star Preston Wilson, Mookie's stepson, along with two others. With the Yankees piling up wins and attention at a record pace, the Mets were a forgotten entity in New York until GM Steve Phillips, after some prodding, landed Piazza from the Marlins. (Florida, in the midst of dismantling a world champion, had acquired him a week earlier from the Dodgers, who demurred on Piazza's contract demands.) After a tremendous 1998, he re-upped for seven more years in New York, which became known as the "Piazza Era."

3. Gary Carter (December 10, 1984)

Though not as defining as the previously mentioned trades, GM Frank Cashen's acquisition of Gary Carter from the Expos for four players—Hubie Brooks being the big piece—assured that the Mets would not be a one-year fluke. Carter was the rarest of breeds: a slugging catcher (see Piazza). What set Carter apart was that he was also one of the game's best defensive backstops with a strong arm, crucial needs given the rookie-dominated staff in New York. Though his Cooperstown plaque has an "M" on the hat, it says "NY" in our hearts. And we'll take the trophy Kid Carter helped pull from the fire in 1986. You'll always be remembered fondly in New York, Kid.

4. Ron Darling and Walt Terrell (April 1, 1982)

This two-for-one deal was controversial at the time. Brooklyn-born Lee Mazzilli, the Mets poster boy—literally—was heartbroken at being sent to Texas for two pitchers still in the minors. "I know the Mets have made some bad deals in the past," Maz said, in grand understatement. "And I want this to become the worst one they ever made." The trade's place on this list is confirmation that it was not. Darling went on to win ninety-nine games as a Met and started three games in the 1986 World Series. Terrell won nineteen games in two full seasons in New York before he was sent to Detroit for slugger Howard Johnson. Maz even came back in 1986 as a key bat off the bench for the world champs. Back in 1982, Manager George Bamberger displayed foresight: "In a few years, the Mets will have the best pitching in the big leagues. That's the way you win." It still is.

5. John Olerud (December 20, 1996)

The separate 1980s deals that brought the Mets Sid Fernandez and David Cone deserve consideration for this spot, but the Olerud deal jump-started the Mets renaissance before the turn of the millennium. Johnny O. was quieter than was Keith Hernandez, but this sweet-swinging lefty with the smooth first baseman's glove was, like Hernandez, a former batting champ and world champ. Among Mets with at least one thousand plate appearances, Olerud is the team's all-time batting and on-base percentage leader in a season and a career—by a wide margin. And the Blue Jays gave Mets GM Joe McIlvaine $5 million to take him in 1996. The Mets sent pitcher Robert Person to Toronto—and their eternal thanks.

◠ Worst Trades ◠

It says something about a franchise when trading "The Franchise" doesn't even rank as its worst deal. Trading Tom Seaver in 1977 brought a lot of ill will, but it also brought four players. The worst trade in club history sent

The Midnight Massacre

Every team has made trades they regretted. A budding star is traded for a veteran who is too soon over the hill. A player undervalued by his own organization is dealt for someone the team has overvalued. Or the club makes a short-term roster maneuver that hamstrings the club in the long term. But the most difficult trade is one in which the team's iconic player is on the block because of impending salary demands. Such decisions were faced by the 2011 Mets and will likely occur again as the team moves forward. The question is still the same as it was half a century ago: What can you get in return that justifies trading your best player? How can the move be justified to the fans? The Midnight Massacre is the biggest such test case in Mets history. It occurred in the days when the salary dump was still a novel concept.

The fateful night of June 15, 1977, was a long time in the making. It all began in the autumn of 1975 when Tom Seaver, coming off his third Cy Young season in seven years, initially asked about a multiyear contract. The Mets demurred, and, in the meantime, an arbitrator and two federal courts told Major League Baseball that teams could renew veteran player contracts for one year but not forever. Free agency was a reality. Now, everything was more complicated—and more expensive.

Negotiations took place in March 1976 in the dingy visitor's clubhouse at the Yankees' spring training facility because Fort Lauderdale was relatively close to Board Chairman M. Donald Grant's Hobe Sound home. Seaver emerged with a three-year contract and an annual base salary of $225,000, plus incentives. The whole process bothered Seaver, as did the fact that inferior pitchers soon wound up getting more money than he did, when they switched teams.

Grant held a patrician attitude toward players who rose above their original station in life. He took exception when Seaver joined old-money Greenwich Country Club, and Grant didn't like that the public thought "The Franchise" was bigger than the franchise itself. Grant had been Joan Payson's stockbroker, but now Payson was dead—as was Gil Hodges. Grant had pushed out thorn-in-his-side Whitey Herzog, who as farm director had helped build the team from farce to force. There was no one to rein in the old man, and Grant was delusional enough to think he was doing what the fans really wanted, never mind that the phones were ringing off the hook begging the team not to trade Seaver.

Seaver finally went over Grant's head to team president Lorinda de Roulet and agreed to an extension for three years and $1 million, which would have lasted through 1981. Yet when *Daily News* columnist Dick Young—now serving as Grant's mouthpiece—blasted Seaver's family the day of the trading deadline, Seaver terminated his handshake deal with the Mets and demanded a trade. The Mets learned about his change of heart during a board meeting in which de Roulet was relaying the specifics of her deal with Seaver.

That the best player in franchise history—then or now—brought back only Doug Flynn, Pat Zachry, Steve Henderson, and Dan Norman, was beyond comprehension. A simultaneous deal with San Diego banished disgruntled slugger Dave Kingman for Bobby Valentine and Paul Siebert. A third trade of Mike Phillips to St. Louis for Joel Youngblood turned out fine in the long run. But no minor trade could make up for the major screwup that sent Seaver out of town. Another seven years in the desert had begun.

away another three-hundred-game winner, and the Mets had to send three players with him just to complete the deal.

1. Nolan Ryan (December 10, 1971)

GM Bob Scheffing traded this future Hall of Famer, strikeouts king, three-hundred-game winner, and no-hit record holder—plus three prospects who were washouts, mercifully for the Mets—for Jim Fregosi, a shortstop the Mets forced to play third base, which he couldn't play. This should stand forever as the worst trade in Mets history. We hope.

2. Amos Otis (December 3, 1969)

Famous Amos ranks so high because the Mets got so little in return for an All-Star who banged out two thousand hits and was one of the game's most dependable center fielders. GM Johnny Murphy also sent hard-throwing-but-troubled right-hander Bob Johnson to the Royals, while the Mets got back even-more-troubled third baseman Joe Foy. Too bad the Mets didn't just give up on third base instead of on Otis and Ryan. (Or they could have just let Wayne Garrett play third without the hassle.)

3. Tom Seaver (June 15, 1977)

This might actually look good as a salary dump today, but let's spell out this deal by GM Joe McDonald: getting Pat Zachry, Steve Henderson, Doug Flynn, and Dan Norman did not equal Seaver, for a year or a career. To illustrate, these four players' Wins Above Replacement over their Mets careers (10.1 combined) was only slightly above Seaver's best WAR season as a Met (9.5 in 1973). It never will add up.

4. Rusty Staub (December 12, 1975)

The scary thing about this trade is that it was one in a long line of bad 1970s deals that started with the dispatching of Amos Otis a month before the 1970s began and ended with the banishing of Jon Matlack and John Milner in December 1978. In between those dates, the Mets exiled almost every beloved ballplayer on the 1969 and 1973 pennant-winning rosters. Because Rusty was about to have enough service time to dictate where he would play, Joe McDonald traded him to Detroit for Mickey Lolich, four years his senior, who retired after one season at Shea.

5. Lenny Dykstra (June 18, 1989)

There are so many other bad trades trying to sneak into the top five, but it's hard to beat this deal—so to speak. GM Frank Cashen's trade with division foe Philadelphia, which included workhorse reliever Roger McDowell, brought back Juan Samuel, a free-swinging strikeout machine playing out of position. All you need to know about what the Mets thought of this deal is that they immediately dumped Samuel after the season.

Free Agents

When the first crop of free agents came on the market in November 1976, the Mets took no part in the tectonic change to the baseball landscape. The next winter they signed minor league pitcher Tom Hausman and Elliot Maddox, an injury-prone utility man. Things haven't gotten much rosier, but a few deals have been beneficial.

Players re-signed by the Mets are not included, so no Mike Piazza—or Oliver Perez and Luis Castillo. Years indicated are the player's first season after signing and the guaranteed portion of each deal.

Best Deals

Carlos Beltran (2005: seven years, $119 million)
The Mets got as much from Carlos as any free agent they've had, though he lost the better part of 2009 and 2010 to injury. Even when they traded him to the Giants in July 2011, Beltran brought back a blue-chip prospect in pitcher Zack Wheeler.

Rick Reed (1996: minor league free agent)
A minor league free agent, but a major find. The former replacement player was instrumental in the 1997 turnaround season and was a superb big-game pitcher.

Robin Ventura (1999: four years, $32 million)
Ventura had one great season in 1999 and was an inspirational leader as well as the best bases-loaded hitter this side of Pat Tabler. He solidified what *Sports Illustrated* thought might be "The Best Infield Ever."

Rickey Henderson (1999: two years, $3.9 million)
Like Ventura, Rickey came along in 1999 and was instrumental in ending an 11-season playoff drought. He gave Queens the last great season of his legendary and nomadic career.

Pedro Martinez (2005: four years, $50 million)
He showed the Mets could attract stars. Pedro had one great year as a Met, but injuries turned him into one great cheerleader.

Worst Deals

Vince Coleman (1991: four years, $12 million)
After Darryl Strawberry was insulted by the Mets offer, the deal Coleman got was an insult to Mets fans. After two and a half miserable seasons in New York, he threw a firecracker at a crowd of people in L.A. He never played for the Mets again.

Bobby Bonilla (1992: five years, $27.5 million)
One of the least-liked Mets ever, Bobby Boo was a Broadway flop whose decent numbers didn't jibe with the agony of watching him daily. He was a bad fit and a brutal fielder.

Roger Cedeno (2002: four years, $18 million)
GM Steve Phillips traded Cedeno at the height of his usefulness and two years later inexplicably signed the slower, chubbier, and far more expensive free agent.

Kaz Matsui (2004: three years, $20 million)
Moving Jose Reyes to second base so this scatter-armed banjo hitter could play short may be as bad a personnel decision as the Mets have made in this millennium.

Jason Bay (2010: four years, $66 million)
This list is an international crow-eating feast with a Venezuelan (Cedeno), a Japanese import (Matsui), and a Canadian (Bay). Jay Bay's decline factored into altering the Citi Field dimensions—plus, his gargantuan salary limits expenditures.

Best Mets Booth

Win or lose, happy recap or gut-wrenching reiteration, Mets fans have always been able to rely on the people who have brought the play-by-play of the team into their homes, cars, bars, ear buds, or even handheld devices. To recap the top-five Mets announcers would essentially leave one member of the best three-man booths out of the listing. So, instead, we bring you the best Mets booths, evaluating the top-five broadcast teams that maintained a professional level and told it like it was, whether on TV or radio or both.

1. Lindsey Nelson, Bob Murphy, and Ralph Kiner on Radio and TV (1962–1978)

Nelson was the big name in this triumvirate, but he left after the Mets entered their second great abyss in the late 1970s. The seventeen seasons they were together still stands as the longest for a broadcasting trio in baseball history. They usually worked with one announcer on radio, one on TV, and the other off. For home games, Kiner usually hung around in the late innings, getting ready for his postgame staple, *Kiner's Korner.*

2. Gary Cohen, Ron Darling, and Keith Hernandez on TV (2006–present)

Cohen, the radio voice of the team since 1989, made the shift over to the TV booth with the launching of SNY in 2006. Hernandez was already a Mets TV personality, and Darling came over that year from Washington. It was a perfect storm: two former teammates plus an ardent Mets fan turned announcer's announcer. Gary, Keith, and Ron became part of the Mets lexicon and even a charitable foundation.

3. Bob Murphy and Gary Cohen on Radio (1989–2003)

A hybrid of the first two groups on the list, the fifteen seasons this pair spent calling Mets games spawned a new generation of Mets fans who listened while driving around in their cars or who listened to WFAN under the covers at night or who sneaked in a forbidden West Coast game long after bedtime—just as previous generations did while listening to Murph. Cohen provided a lot of new thrills, "It's outta here!" And Murph made the new feel like old times again, "The Mets win the ballgame."

4. Gary Cohen and Howie Rose on Radio (2004–2005)

Love for a baseball team is inspired on TV, enhanced in person, and forged on the radio. That is how Cohen and Rose were raised as Mets fans, and, in their two seasons together, they instilled into people that they weren't just listening to a mediocre team's games; they were a part of something greater. Rose left a crowded Mets cable TV booth to anchor the radio booth and essentially replace the irreplaceable Bob Murphy (Howie still anchors the radio side). When Murph died suddenly in 2004, Cohen and Rose were like nephews telling the family about the legacy of their beloved great uncle.

5. Ralph Kiner and Tim McCarver on TV (1983–1998)

Before McCarver became a ubiquitous presence for every national game and adopted the propensity for belaboring a point, he was a top-notch announcer for the Mets. In fact, he even raised Kiner's game after Ralph and Bob Murphy were split up, with Murph moved to radio full-time. McCarver knew how to take the Kiner stories about the old days and liven them up while utilizing the Hall of Fame slugger's insights. In time, this pair only worked non-cable games until the Mets replaced McCarver with Tom Seaver in 1999.

⚾ Best Mets Coaches ⚾

The Mets have had some ninety men serve as coaches, and that does not even take into account all the bullpen catchers and batting practice pitchers. (The team media guide usually lists them all, if you're desperate to know.) Rather than list all of them, here's a Mets coaching staff you'd go to war with.

Batting Coach: Willie Mays (Mets coach, 1974–1979)

Many people say a batting coach at the major league level is overrated. Whether that is true or not, having the Say Hey Kid in charge of hitting makes sense here. He hit 660 home runs, knocked in 1,903, and had 3,283 hits. He might be a help to the outfielders, too.

Pitching Coach: Rube Walker (1968–1981)

The former Brooklyn Dodgers catcher came over with Gil Hodges from Washington, and Rube devised the concept of the five-man pitching rotation to help nurse the best pitching staff in franchise history to a world championship in 1969. He lasted through five managers, so he must have done something right.

Pitching Coach: Mel Stottlemyre (1984–1993)

One thing Rube wasn't, however, was a pitcher. Nolan Ryan complained about it when he was traded, and if you're going to create an all-time coaching staff, you want to retroactively make a Hall of Famer happy and keep him in New York. So Mel, who had been a solid pitcher in his day as a Yankee, makes the team as a second pitching coach. (On this squad, he can toss BP.) Stottlemyre did a good job with the second-best pitching staff in franchise history and helped them claim a world championship.

First-Base Coach: Mookie Wilson (1997–2002, 2011)

Some would question the importance of a first-base coach. But if you had to pick one, why wouldn't you pick Mookie? Sorry, Bill Robinson.

Third-Base Coach: Eddie Yost (1968–1975)

"And along the lines at third is 'The Walking Man,' Eddie Yost." That's how Lindsey Nelson regularly introduced the white-haired coach who arrived from Washington with Gil Hodges—as did Rube Walker and Joe Pignatano.

Yost got his nickname for the staggering 1,614 walks he drew, leading the American League six times in the 1950s. Yost could also coax runs out of the stingy Mets offense with the judicious waving of his arm. He left for Boston in 1976 because the Mets front office lowballed him.

Name: Meet the Burros?

From day one, New York's expansion team was the team of the people. Out of 9,613 suggestions, a list of 644 names was formed. It was whittled down to a top ten in February 1961. Drum roll, please . . .

Avengers
Bees
Burros
Continentals
Jets
Metropolitans
NYBs
Rebels
Skyliners
Skyscrapers

Meadowlarks—owner Joan Payson's pick and not a bad name compared to a few—didn't even make the cut. Also denied were names later taken by three future major league sports teams: Devils, Islanders, and Nationals. Tough crowd.

Board Chairman M. Donald Grant announced Mets as the official name at the Savoy Hilton Hotel on May 8, 1961. Mets had been the name of the American Association champions of 1885 before the club dissolved three years later. But in a new century with a "New Breed," "Mets" fit nicely in a headline and sounded an awful lot like the franchise's legal name—New York Metropolitan Baseball Club, Inc. Besides, the 287 votes it received beat every other name. Payson followed the will of the people, and the people followed the team through hell and high water.

Bench Coach: Whitey Herzog (1966)

You take a Hall of Fame manager as your bench coach if he's available. Herzog only coached for a year because he got kicked upstairs to the front office—partly because Manager Wes Westrum saw him as a threat. He was darned right. If the Mets had kept Herzog in the dugout, he may well have replaced Westrum, and, perhaps, Gil Hodges wouldn't have become manager in New York. But Herzog could never stand Board Chairman M. Donald Grant, so there goes that theory.

Bullpen Coach: Joe Pignatano (1968–1982)

While fellow original Met Al Jackson gets consideration for the spot, Piggy gets the nod for one main reason: He started the tomato plants in the bullpen. End of story.

Table 5.3.   Ownership Comparison

	Paysons	*Wilpons*
First Gained Stake in Ownership	1962[a]	1980[b]
Seasons Owned	18	32
Years until First Winning Season	7	6
NL Pennants	2	2
World Championships	1	1
First-Place Finishes	2	3
Last-Place Finishes	8	5
Managers (including interim)[c]	8	13
General Managers	5	7
Highest Attendance	2.69 million (1970)	4.04 million (2008)
Uniform Numbers Retired	2	2[d]
Stadiums	Polo Grounds, Shea Stadium	Shea Stadium, Citi Field
Purchase Price	$3.75 million	$21.1 million

[a] Payson ownership actually dates to 1961; 1962 is used to signify her first baseball season as owner.

[b] Majority of purchase price was paid and controlled by Doubleday Publishing. Nelson Doubleday sold his company in 1986, and he and the Wilpons became equal partners. The Wilpons purchased Doubleday's shares in 2002.

[c] Joe Torre is counted as manager for both ownership regimes.

[d] Includes number 42 retired throughout baseball for Jackie Robinson at Shea Stadium ceremony.

Mets People

Pete Flynn: "Keeper of the Field"

Even if you're not familiar with Pete Flynn, you know the man's work. He's no relation to Mets second baseman Doug Flynn (1977–1981), but Pete's manicured infield helped Doug win a Gold Glove in 1980. Nineteen Gold Gloves were doled out to Mets at Shea Stadium, a tribute to those players and also to the man charged with keeping baseball's most maligned ballpark looking good.

> *"If you throw a full beer and hit somebody with it, you could kill him."*

The Mets groundskeeper has seen it all, cared for it all, and cleaned it all up. Flynn, who officially retired and was honored by the team before the last game of 2011, swept up a sewage leak the day the place opened in 1964 and collected debris heaved at Pete Rose in left field after his fabled fight with Bud Harrelson in 1973. "There was a Jack Daniels bottle out there," Flynn recalled on a summer afternoon before going to work at Citi Field. "A lot of beer cans. Shortly after that I think they put a stop to [selling cans to fans], that way they couldn't throw them out [at opposing players]. If you throw a full beer and hit somebody with it, you could kill him." Vendors started pouring cans of beer into cups.

Shea has always been adaptive, but Shea has never been busier than it was in 1975. The Mets, Jets, Yankees, and Giants all played home games at Shea that year because of the reconstruction of Yankee Stadium: 173 games in all that year at the big Shea. The overwork put Flynn in the hospital, but he was soon back in shape—as was his field.

The red-bearded, twinkle-eyed Irishman kept the field in top condition despite all the tenants and the city's fiscal crisis, which prevented major improvements during the 1970s. The Shea Stadium head groundskeeper's most challenging task—other than putting up with the stench of the mascot Mettle the Mule in 1979—was repairing the field five different times after it was destroyed by fans: three times in 1969 (the NL East, NLCS, and World Series clinchings), once for capturing the 1973 pennant, and after the Mets won the division title in 1986. The last one was probably the toughest. "We had a day game the next day," Flynn lamented. While the Mets starters all took that day off, the field had to show up, and his crew worked through the night to make it playable. New York City, which put more than $30 million into Shea in the 1980s, ensured that no future looting in the name of celebration took place there. When the Mets won the World Series on October 27, 1986, the players celebrated on the field and the fans cheered in the stands—a wall of police making sure it stayed that way.

By then, half of Flynn's worries had moved to New Jersey. Jets owner Leon Hess, citing the dirty bathrooms, bolted for the Meadowlands after the Jets had called Shea home for twenty seasons. Though the grounds crew no longer needed to convert the field from baseball to football, concerts tore up the field so badly that musical acts were kept out of Shea for eleven years, until Bruce Springsteen's 2003 shows. Billy Joel played the final two concerts there in July 2008, and Flynn, as always, prepared the field for baseball again.

A member of the Irish American Baseball Hall of Fame—along with Tug McGraw—one of Flynn's grandest moments was driving the Beatles to their waiting armored car after the fabled 1965 concert. Flynn, who retired as head groundskeeper in his seventies but, out of habit, remained on the Citi Field grounds crew, drove Paul McCartney on the field for the first concert at the new stadium in 2009. McCartney chuckled when Flynn explained he'd been his Shea driver in 1965—a moment both light and momentous shared by a couple of Shea originals.

CHAPTER **6**

Best Mets Activities

☾ Of Banner Days and Giveaways ☾

F I MAY SAY, there are many things to know and do that make the Mets fan experience unique. One that is not exclusive to Mets fans is perhaps the most basic: going to ballgames.

Some Mets fans started going to see the team play in person at such a young age that they have no eureka moment of being at the ballgame for the first time—of walking through the portal in the Shea upper deck and seeing the expanse of green field, red seats, and blue sky. It is that kind of recollection that lives on long after the razing of the place where those memories were first stirred.

And what could be better than being at the ballgame? Getting free stuff.

The Mets have given out enough promotional merchandise to fill both Shea and Citi Field several times over. Batting helmets, batting gloves, baseball hats, jackets, bats, and bags were handed out at Shea in the days when you didn't have to worry about twenty thousand people beating you to the park and getting all the free stuff. The Doubleday-Wilpon group brought Grucci family fireworks to Shea, and these Fireworks Nights were among the few sellouts the team had in the early 1980s. But you couldn't take the "oohs" and "aahs" of the bombs bursting in air with you like you could, say, a calendar or a pair of flip-flops. The latter was a one-time giveaway in 1984. These "shower shoes" as Tim McCarver called them in the countless

155

promos leading up to the June 2 game against the Cardinals, littered the field as a tribute to Hubie Brooks after his last at bat signaled the end of his record twenty-four-game hitting streak.

A pitcher and four tumblers on Memorial Day 1988 were perfect for pouring out refreshment during a rain delay against the Dodgers. Too bad the beer prices—a preposterous $2.25 a cup back then—made the pitcher the most expensive pour in the tristate area.

Nostalgia tinged the 1990s giveaways as some of the best-remembered promotions were for clubs long gone. Negro League cap day was both stylish and educational. A New York Giants and Brooklyn Dodgers cap giveaway—the fan got to take his or her pick—could have been called "Teams That Abandoned New York Cap Day." After the 1994 strike, the merchandise improved, the effort increased, and better quality Mets items made its way from China to Flushing. Artwork, commemorative pins, sunglasses, and Beanie Babies took fans through the early Bobby Valentine years and the home run chase when it seemed suddenly quite normal that everyone and his brother was hitting fifty home runs.

The Mets gave out flags in 2001—first, little white flags (how appropriate) announcing their 2000 pennant but nothing about their loss to the Yankees. And when everything changed and people filed into Shea for the first time after the World Trade Center catastrophe, American flags were distributed. Americans celebrating their ethnic heritage became an August staple, though it was often more about mood and food than about giveaways, with some exceptions. Festival Latina and Meringue Night featured postgame concerts, as did Irish Night, which often included a green Mets hat giveaway, concerts by the likes of Black 47, and sometimes even a complimentary bar of Irish Spring upon exiting. One sweaty fan stared at the soap silently placed in his hand: "I think I've just been insulted."

But along the way with the myriad of bobbleheads, shirts, hats, bags, caps, and cups, the events that merited no souvenir passed by the boards. You can still see these special days highlighted on SNY in *Mets Yearbook* (the renamed highlight films of the old days). Camera Day, Family Day, Oldtimer's Day were pushed off the calendar in favor of free swag. But one day gone missing leaves a bigger void than do the rest.

Banner Day was part of the Mets' afterbirth. The sheer love the early fans had for their hapless players and the brutal team they played for is what inspired these bedsheet confessions that sprang up all over the club's first home, the Polo Grounds. Casey Stengel called them "placards" and it was the first manager's ability to point to the stands instead of toward his bench that was the true genius behind the early Mets. Stengel had debuted in the major leagues half a century earlier, he had won more pennants in less time than anyone in history during his dozen years with the Yankees, and he knew that the expansion Mets had the makings of being the worst team in history. He was right. He was confounded and confounded others with his own language, Stengelese: "You'd think we'd do better and without all these people turning out with the banners and cheers and it's 'Metsie, Metsie, Metsie.'"

"We don't want to set the world on fire—we just want to finish ninth."

Banner Day entrant, mid-1960s

It didn't make sense. It didn't have to. Banners filled the Polo Grounds. At first, team president George Weiss wanted to confiscate the scrawled-on bed sheets, but Weiss was eventually convinced that the people paying good money to see a bad club should have their fun. The Mets weren't the Yankees. And the Mets fans delighted in bringing their banners with them for the first Mayor's Trophy Game at Yankee Stadium in 1963. The Mets won the game and outlasted the ushers in the Bronx, who kept confiscating the bed sheets. The team rewarded the fans with the first Banner Day on September 15. The last doubleheader ever played at the ancient Polo Grounds, a twinbill with Houston, was the first in a long line of double-headers acknowledging the fans' rights to express themselves—they were allowed on the field to do so between games. Fitting with the theme, the Mets obediently lost both games. One of the four hundred banners that day read: "Know why the Mets are the best losers in the league?—Practice makes perfect."

The ability to laugh at one's self and have fun even in trying times remained a hallmark of the Mets. The Banner Day tradition moved to a new place, Shea Stadium. It became one of the most popular days of the season, with the people charging money for admission allowing the patrons to provide the entertainment. The annual fan parade went on from the Amazin'

Mets of Gil Hodges to the awful Mets of Joe Torre, through the team's blossoming in the mid-1980s. A second Banner Day was added, in 1991, with a military theme following the Gulf War. But the homey tradition of Banner Day became trapped in the changing logistics and economics of the game. Sunday, August 14, 1988, was the last scheduled doubleheader for Banner Day. That twinbill started at noon so as not to interfere too much with the travel schedule of the players, because the banner portion added at least an hour to the proceedings. For financial reasons, by 1988, doubleheaders were rarely scheduled. Two-for-one admissions went the way of Camera Day.

Banner Day was held for another eight seasons, but the kick people got out of it was the thrill of sitting in the stands—or sitting at home and watching on TV—with nothing better to do. You've paid for and witnessed one game, you'll soon get another game for free, and there's a free show of ingenuity and enthusiasm in front of you as hundreds and often thousands of banners parade across the field, all with variations of the same theme: "We love the Mets."

Will Citi Field see a Banner Day? You never can tell. As cool as Banner Day was, fans would rather see a world championship banner flying over the place someday. As a banner from Bensonhurst or Bellport or Bayonne invariably said: "We'll believe it when we see it. Let's go Mets!"

⚾ Mr. Met Dash ⚾

The Mr. Met Dash is a Mets tradition dating back to the mid-1990s. Formerly called "Dyna-Mets Dash" and "Kids Dash," among other things, it has been renamed after the club's large-noggined-but-silent mascot and allows kids to run the bases after selected games. (Senior citizens and adult season-ticket holders receive the occasional opportunity to stroll around the field as well.) The jaunt begins at first base and ends with touching home plate, but there's more to the exercise than dashing—or walking—270 feet.

People who want to participate in a Mr. Met Dash, which is generally held on scattered Sunday afternoons during the season, should go to the right-field entrance sometime after the seventh inning and start lining up outside the ballpark. The earlier you get in line, the sooner you'll get inside to run the bases, but keep in mind, the running won't begin until almost half an hour after the game ends. Bring liquids, hats, food, reading mate-rial, activity books, and a radio—or a phone—if you want to follow how the game ends. The line can snake all the way out to the 7-line platform, which, thankfully, provides shade, because that commodity is in short sup-ply during the wait.

Once the line gets going, you'll go back through the right-field en-trance, leading you past the bullpen and onto the field. Taking pictures on the warning track of kids crashing into the wall is usually all right, as long as the line keeps moving. When it's time for your loved ones to run the bases, one parent should be stationed near home plate (ideally to the right of home plate for the best angle). Take more than one picture of the little ones crossing home plate because someone will invariably be standing in front of you.

And then you're done. Everyone in the family may essentially be "done" by then. It will have been a full day. Even Mr. Met looks a little pooped by the end of his dash.

☺ Go to a Mets Road Game ☺

More and more Mets fans choose to see their team play in other locales and call it a vacation. It is also a way to go to a city that you wouldn't normally go to. There's something to be said about going to another team's ballpark when you have no rooting interest, but here's one man's recommendations for the best National League cities to visit in your Metsian travels. For more detail or to plan your own trip, check out ballparkeguides.com or one of the many books or sites on contemporary ballparks.

San Francisco

The ballpark is the best of the new National League parks, and it's actually bigger and more expensive than is Citi Field, so you should feel right at home. As a city, San Francisco is hard to top. If you have kids, take a trol-ley ride. If you have a date, go to Fisherman's Wharf. If you're married, try Alcatraz. (Couldn't leave that one alone.)

Suggested Side Trip: Monterrey. The aquarium alone is worth the trip. The scenery and the scene is splendid, and you can look out the car window and see where much of your food is grown.

Chicago

Wrigley Field is the best ballpark in the major leagues. It is even worth putting up with some of the more abrasive and intoxicated Cubs fans you're likely to find there. Warning: While most of the world has forgotten the Miracle Mets of 1969, the wound is still fresh in Chicago, even for twenty-somethings whose parents were in kindergarten at the time.

Suggested Side Trip: The Field Museum or the Lincoln Park Zoo is great if you have kids. The Art Institute of Chicago is worth going to if you're interested in art or in giving the impression that you're about more than baseball. Taking the elevator to the top of the Hancock Tower is a nice way to see the city if you don't have the time or the inclination to walk it—and if it's not cloudy or crowded.

Philadelphia

Probably the most economical trip is to Philadelphia, but you get what you pay for. Getting tickets is difficult, but they may be cheaper than tickets at Citi Field. When the two teams are competitive at the same time—which in fifty years has happened in only 2007 and 2008—there can be some rough interplay between the fan bases. The food is good and the stadium is nice, though it's somewhat reminiscent of New York's new NL ballpark.

Suggested Side Trip: Valley Forge. You think Mets fans have suffered? Check out the cabins the Continental Army called home in the winter of 1777–1778. Yes, there is shopping nearby.

Pittsburgh

Many people love PNC Park, yet the Pirates consistently draw among the fewest fans in the game (must be a Pirate thing). The park has plenty to keep fans entertained, even during the most lopsided ballgame. The sight-lines are great, as is the food. Get there by walking the bridge and check out the massive Honus Wagner, Roberto Clemente, Bill Mazeroski, and Willie Stargell statues, and try to figure out how the great Ralph Kiner rates only a sculpture of a pair of hands. Then order an Iron City.

Suggested Side Trip: It's a long drive from New York to Pittsburgh, so you might want to stay put once you get there. You can spend the better part of a day in Pittsburgh just visiting places named after Andrew Carnegie. The Children's Museum of Pittsburgh is also recommended.

Houston

It's easier to ignore the short porch in left and Tal's Hill in center when you're there in person. The food is excellent, and that retractable roof can come in handy if you're there after early May and the humidity takes control. There is plenty of nightlife not far from the park.

Suggested Side Trip: Austin is a couple of hours away, and the university town has plenty to appeal to conservatives and liberals alike. On the way there, stop at Whataburger. Yes, it's a burger chain with a dumb name, but you'll thank me.

☾ Minor Mets ☾

Seeing the Mets in a minor league setting can be fun if you're blessed to live near such a spot. If you're not, a visit every once in a while to the smaller burgs and ballparks can be good for the soul. A couple of favorite Mets minor league haunts have long since moved on—notably Pittsfield and Lynchburg—but anything that gets you to see beautiful Savannah has to be worthwhile. Here's information on Mets affiliates through 2011 that might help speed a minor journey.

Buffalo Bisons

Class: AAA.

Affiliate Since: 2009.

Season Length: Early April through Labor Day.

Types of Players: Players sent down from the majors or those a call away from a spot in the big leagues. Some never make the final step.

Stadium: Coca-Cola Park.

Capacity: 18,025.

Address: 275 Washington Street, Buffalo, New York 14203.

Phone: 716-846-2000.

Website: www.bisons.com.

Binghamton Mets

Class: AA.

Affiliate Since: 1992.

Season Length: Early April through Labor Day.

Types of Players: Prospects almost always join B-Mets before heading to the majors. Some never stop at AAA.

Stadium: NYSEG Stadium.

Capacity: 6,012.

Address: 211 Henry Street, Binghamton, New York 13901.

Phone: 607-723-6387.

Website: www.bmets.com.

St. Lucie Mets

Class: A.

Affiliate Since: 1988.

Season Length: Early April through Labor Day.

Types of Players: Top prospects stop here. Many major leaguers rehabbing injuries also come to the facility that hosts spring training. (Warning: The hill seating area in the outfield is often closed during the minor league season.)

Stadium: Digital Domain Park.

Capacity: 7,400.

Address: 525 NW Peacock Blvd., Port St. Lucie, Florida 34986.

Phone: 772-871-2115.

Website: www.stluciemets.com.

Savannah Sand Gnats

Class: A.

Affiliate Since: 2007.

Season Length: Early April through Labor Day.

Types of Players: Usually players who've been in the organization for one or more years and have played in the Gulf Coast or Dominican League. Advanced prospects might wind up here quickly.

Stadium: Grayson Stadium.

Capacity: 8,000.

Address: 1401 East Victory Drive, Savannah, Georgia 31404.

Phone: 912-351-9150.

Website: www.sandgnats.com.

Brooklyn Cyclones

Class: A (Short Season).

Affiliate Since: 2001.

Season Length: Mid-June through Labor Day.

Types of Players: A showcase spot because of its location, advanced draft picks from college often make their first pro stop here on the ladder through the system. Rehabbing major leaguers also appear occasionally.

Stadium: MCU Park.

Capacity: 7,500.

Address: 1904 Surf Avenue, Brooklyn, New York 11224.

Phone: 718-449-8497.

Website: www.brooklyncyclones.com.

Kingsport Mets

Class: A (Rookie).

Affiliate Since: 1980.

Season Length: Mid-June through late August.

Types of Players: Players drafted from high school, coming from Gulf Coast League, or Dominican League often end up as K-Mets.

Stadium: Hunter Wright Stadium.

Capacity: 2,000.

Address: 800 Granby Road, Kingsport, Tennessee 37665.

Phone: 423-378-3744.

Website: www.kmets.com.

Gulf Coast League Mets

Class: A (Rookie).

Affiliate Since: 1991.

Season Length: Mid-June through late August.

Types of Players: Players deemed raw, went undrafted, are coming off injuries, or playing in the United States for the first time. Games are often played in a back field in the Port St. Lucie complex. No admission is charged, but most games start at noon during middle of day in summer.

Dominican League Mets

Class: A (Rookie).
Affiliate Since: 1993.
Season Length: End of May through late August.
Types of Players: The Mets actually have two teams in this league (they formerly had a team in Venezuela). The best players from these teams will venture to Florida and begin their trek up the big league ladder.
Stadium: Estadio Quisqueya.
Address: Calle Frank Felix Miranda #1 ENS, Naco Santo Domingo, Dominican Republic.
Phone: 809-567-3090.
Website: www.minorleaguebaseball.com/clubs/ip_index.jsp?sid=milb&cid =t620.

⚾ Cyber Mets ⚾

The Internet is truly where the game never ends. Blogs allow Mets fans to obsess about their club any hour of the day or night. While it's nigh on impossible to get an accurate count of blogs about the Mets, the consensus from talking to several is that there are probably as many as one hundred different Mets-centric sites, including metsilverman.com, where the story continues after this book is closed.

With that gratuitous plug out of the way, here's the pressing question for some of the better bloggers: Why is blogging about the Mets so popular?

It is a never-ending soap opera. Imagine a blog in 1986–1987? "Yay, we won the World Series! Hey, why wasn't Gooden at the parade? Oh, he overslept. Oh, wait, he didn't oversleep. Knight isn't coming back? Wow, everyone is hurt. Seaver might come back!" If you can't think of anything to write about just wait two hours and the Mets will provide fodder.

—Shannon Shark, Mets Police (metspolice.com)

It's New York, which is full of people who love baseball and people who want to be writers. I think it's that the Yankees are the default choice for what to be a fan of in New York. Tradition, huge payroll, world championships, blah, blah, blah. If you're a writer type, you've probably got a streak of the romantic in you—and that romanticism doesn't harmonize with rooting for a team that's the favorite to win the World Series every year.

—Jason Fry and Greg Prince, Faith and Fear in Flushing (faithandfearinflushing.com)

I've always believed blogging is a kind of Banner Day for the digital age. Mets fans have always been good at finding ways to express themselves, and the Internet is a great tool.

—Jon Springer, Mets by the Numbers (mbtn.net)

I think there's some sort of inherent frustration in being a Mets fan—maybe because of the presence of the Yankees—and it prompts people to fret about the team in a unique way. . . . There's an element of drama running throughout the team's history—again, perhaps fueled by being the little-brother franchise in a big, big town—that invites daily chronicling.

—Ted Berg, Ted Quarters (tedquarters.net)

Mets fans are some of the most passionate baseball fans around. So naturally the fans want to talk about their team and what better way to do so then by creating your own forum (a blog). There are probably more Mets blogs out there than for any other baseball team.

—Kerel Cooper, On the Black (ontheblack.com)

For me, reliving the Mets days of the 1960s, early 1970s is my favorite thing to write about. It brings me back to a time where the Mets were everything, maybe not the best players of all time, but they were our guys.

—Louie Maz, Centerfield Maz (centerfieldmaz.com)

I think blogging the Mets is so popular because it's usually such a painful and dramatic experience to follow this team. . . . Maybe there's a touch of narcissism among Mets fans as well, a feeling that our opinions should be shared with the world.

—Dave Doyle, The Mets Report (metsreport.com)

⚾ Best Mets Bars ⚾

So you're looking for a place to watch the Mets game where you won't be hassled. We'll try to find you a table.

There are countless choices, but we're trying to hit those in geographic areas where Mets fans might find themselves in need of company. A choice so obvious it's not even included in the list proper is **McFadden's Pub**, located adjacent to Citi Field on the center-field side of the ballpark. It has good drink specials, entertaining drink servers, and is guaranteed to have plenty of Mets fans at any given time.

Below is a look at Mets bars that are not so obvious. These are based on experience, not solicitations, so an attempt is being made not to sound like a commercial. When you enjoy a place, though, it sometimes comes out sounding that way.

The Pine Restaurant (Corona, New York)

It's a restaurant and watering hole located at the Holiday Inn LaGuardia, about a ten-minute walk from the ballpark. Because it's so close to the airport, there are always lots of people from other locales adding to the mix (Mets players in the process of finding long-term accommodations can also sometimes be spotted). If you are in from out of town to see the game, or celebrating a Mets victory a little too vociferously, Holiday Inn LGA is a nice place to lay your head as well. The Pine used to be a Bobby Valentine's restaurant back in the good old days when he was still the skipper.

Address: 37-10 114th Street, Corona, 718-651-2100; www.holidaylga.com/dining/pine-restaurant/.

Best Mets Lit

Settle down, class. Welcome to the first day of your major in Mets literature. We have a lot of ground to cover, so let's get right to the reading list.

Mets 101

The Complete Year by Year NY Mets Fan's Almanac by Duncan Bock and John Jordan (1992)

This book breaks down each of the first thirty seasons in Mets history, detailing events not just with the team but regarding the world and culture as well. It even has Shea price indexes year by year for ballpark staples through 1991. It's an indispensable guide and an excellent introduction into the genre.

Can't Anyone Here Play This Game by Jimmy Breslin (1963)

Baseball is serious but the Mets are fun. This is still the funniest book ever written about the Mets. It was penned as the implausibly bad 1962 season was happening, and Breslin's prose frames every subsequent retrospective on the original 120-loss Mets as comedy rather than tragedy.

Mets Fan by Dana Brand (2007)

This is the most unique look behind the jolly, fragile, agitated, animated mask worn by the Mets fan. The late author, a one-of-a-kind teacher, fan, and person, defines fandom and gets to the heart of what following a team is all about, as illogical and time-consuming as it may seem—though no one has ever used either adjective when discussing 1969 or 1986.

200-Level Course Load

The New York Mets by Leonard Koppett (1973 edition)

This *New York Times* beat writer was with the team from day one and insightfully contemplates the humor, the irony, the sorrow, the pity, and the sheer, unadulterated joy of the first dozen seasons in Mets history.

If at First by Keith Hernandez and Mark Bryan (1985)

If you want to know what it's like to rule a city from a seat in the locker room, if you want to know what it's like to go from the depths of a slump to the delights of a streak, if you want to select the finest wood for your personally prepared bats or the finest cocktail for your postgame prowl, if you want to know what it's like to be at your lowest and receive a standing ovation from fifty thousand people in the heat of a pennant race . . . *If at First*.

Screwball by Tug McGraw and Joseph Durso (1974)

Compare and contrast the works of McGraw and Hernandez and how society allowed these two Northern Californian iconoclasts to tell similar stories in dissimilar ways a decade apart. Use front and back of sheet for your answer.

The Worst Team Money Could Buy by Bob Klapisch and John Harper (1993)

This is what happens when you don't have the likes of Hernandez or McGraw in the locker room or on the field. The title refers to the 1992 team, but it could also apply to the direct by-product: the 1993 team that lost thirteen more games and looked even uglier.

300-Level Course Load

The New York Mets: Twenty-Five Years of Baseball Magic by Jack Lang and Eric Simon (1986)

This book is similar to the Koppett book, except Lang includes more detail and images, plus he covers an additional dozen seasons. As Mets beat writer for the *Long Island Press* and then the *New York Daily News*, Lang not only covered the news, he was sometimes a part of the story. He fought the good fight to combat the spew by Dick Young to try to keep Seaver in New York in 1977, and he was blamed by M. Donald Grant for forcing them to trade Nolan Ryan.

Pedro, Carlos, and Omar by Adam Rubin (2006)

It's interesting how the Mets put all sorts of restraints on previous general manager Jim Duquette and then gave his replacement, Omar Minaya, a blank checkbook. Here's the inside look from an insightful beat guy during one of the major transitional seasons in Mets history.

The Bad Guys Won by Jeff Pearlman (2004)

To quote the philoso-miser C. Montgomery Burns, "It's not all hams and plaques." The 1986 Mets famously won the World Series with a last-ditch effort, but what's truly Amazin' is how it happened with half the team dealing with persistent hangovers. That in itself explains how a team built for the ages won only one championship.

A Magic Summer by Stanley Cohen (2009 reissue)

The 1969 Mets were kids who had never experienced success—and many never would again. Cohen, a superb writer, tracked down all but one 1969 Met, and they explain, in their own words, how they did it and what it did for them and for the city.
Extra credit: Rent the film *Frequency* and write a five-hundred-word essay on the joys of shoe polish and ham radio.

Mets by the Numbers by Jon Springer and Matthew Silverman (2008)

Since there is some math involved in this major, we're going to keep it related to the subject matter—and related to the instructor. This book tells the story of every player in Mets history by uniform number, with statistical leaders by uniform number, as well. For updates since first publication, go to mbtn.net. Bonus credit for superlatives about the clever writing.

400-Level Course Load

The Complete Game by Ron Darling with Daniel Paisner (2009)

This is a doctoral thesis on how to approach pitching, written in an entertaining and insightful manner. Required reading in order to graduate or for anyone wanting to move on to the pitching mound or broadcast booth.

The Ticket Out by Michael Sokolove (2004)

This is a detailed look at the players on Darryl Strawberry's supremely talented Crenshaw High School baseball team. Strawberry's life beyond baseball has seen remarkable highs and crashing lows with numerous shots at redemption and multimillion dollar paydays. Imagine what life was like for those who didn't make it big.

The Last Days of Shea by Dana Brand (2009)

The title is self-explanatory. As for the content, I will defer to Dr. Koosman: "When I read Dana Brand's books, I feel as if I'm learning about the heart and soul of the Mets fan. *The Last Days of Shea* is a great tribute to Shea Stadium and to the spirit of the fans who made it such a wonderful place to play baseball."

Faith and Fear in Flushing by Greg Prince (2009)

Like Dr. Brand, Prince gets at the heart of the Mets fan. Prince, who has an encyclopedic memory and an ability to interpret all things in a Metsian universe, tells the story of the team and the fan simultaneously. It is sheer genius in its scope and breadth.

New York Mets: The Complete Illustrated History by Matthew Silverman (2011)

The faculty choice in the recent flurry of coffee table fiftieth-anniversary books, this will be taught in Perfessor Stengel's class. You'll need a thorough textbook with lots of pictures.

Best Mets by Matthew Silverman (2012)

Oh, I see, you already have this book in your hands. Well, then write an essay on what addendums you would make to the various lists and chapters as improvements. Send your answers to the faculty lounge, care of matt@metsilverman.com.

That's tonight's homework. I'll see you tomorrow. Class dismissed.

Bobby V.'s Sports Gallery and Café (Stamford, Connecticut)

It's hard not to have nice things to say about Bobby Valentine's in Stamford, especially after living in the town for a few years. He used to own several other restaurants, but now it's just the Stamford original and another in Arlington, Texas. He sticks to a formula that works: lots of memorabilia, cold beer, and good food. Depending on his schedule, you might even run into Bobby V.
Address: 225 Main Street, Stamford, 203-348-0010; www.bobbyv.com.

Valentine's (Albany, New York)

Not to be confused with Bobby Valentine's, this Albany joint is a Mets haven in the midst of Yankeeland. The people who put together the lively documentary about Mets fans, *Mathematically Alive*, chose Valentine's for their after-party a few years back and introduced an underground Mets world in the state capital. It also features cranking live music despite the place not being huge. The slogan: "We're all about the chin music." They sell Schaefer in a can at prices so cheap, you'd think an old Shea vendor just pulled one out of the tray for you.
Address: 17 Scotland Avenue, Albany, 518-432-6572; www.valentines albany.com.

Phoenix Bar (New York, New York)

New York is a big place, so we list two bars. This Upper East Side establishment gets chosen for its Mets and Jets neon in the window and liberal happy hour. Not your cup of tea? I hear there's about ten thousand other watering holes to choose from in NYC.
Address: 206 East Sixty-seventh Street, between Second and Third Aves., 212-717-8181; www.phoenixparkny.com.

Two Boots Tavern (New York, New York)

There are several locations of this li'l pizza chain. The one referenced here is a cozy spot at Grand Central, but it still manages to get the Mets out. Two Boots has hosted several Mets blogger/writer events, usually held on "Amazin' Tuesday." Geography is how it got its name, in reference to the

melding of boot-shaped Italy and Louisiana that inspired Cajun pizza. Be patient—Mets fans should know how—because it's small. So have a beer, schmooze, and check out the Mets paraphernalia while you're waiting.
Address: Grand Central Terminal, Lower Dining Concourse, New York, 212-557-7992; www.twoboots.com

Duffy's Sports Grill (Port St. Lucie West, Florida)

This also serves as an addendum for the spring training list. This is a chain on the west coast of Florida, but the one you're seeking is the "Superplay," which includes bowling alleys and batting cages. The place is huge, the food is good, it's kid friendly, and the menu is more varied than you'd expect. You might run into anybody there during spring training because Port St. Lucie isn't all that big.
Address: 1600 Northwest Courtyard Circle, Port St. Lucie, 772-408-5800; www.duffyssportsgrill.com.

⚾ Spring Training ⚾

While some fans take trips to see the Mets play on the road, an even larger contingent makes pilgrimages to Florida for spring training. In fact, there is a sizable group that lives in Port St. Lucie due to its proximity to the Mets spring training facility at 525 Northwest Peacock Boulevard. There is also the added bonus of having the team's top Class A club—as well as the site for many major league rehab assignments—right in town all summer. But spring is where it's at in St. Lucie.

Still, the spring used to be a little more exciting before other teams started relocating to Florida's west coast or moving out of the Grapefruit League altogether to spend March in Arizona's Cactus League. Wilpon real estate holdings in neighboring Tradition, Florida, along with a stadium lease that runs through 2018 should keep the Mets at Digital Domain Park (a corporate mouthful of a name for a visual-effects studio). Who is left for the Mets to play that does not require at least a two-hour bus ride is a more pertinent question than whether the Mets are happy at their present digs. The Mets sharing the facility with another major league team is a possibility, though no team has been so targeted. The Mets shared a facility in St. Petersburg with the Cardinals from 1962 until they moved to St. Lucie in 1988.

Mets Conference Call

Mets fans take their baseball seriously—so seriously, in fact, that a leading educational institution put together a three-day conference in honor of the team's fiftieth anniversary. Organized by Hofstra University professors Richard J. Puerzer and the late Dana Brand, it broke new ground as the first multidisciplinary conference to consider every aspect of a Major League Baseball franchise. Speakers and panelists range from authors to journalists to broadcasters to baseball executives. Dedicated to the memory of Dr. Brand, who, besides being former chair of English at Hofstra, created his own subgenre with two books (*Mets Fan* and *The Last Days of Shea*) about the team he followed passionately from its 1962 inception. The conference schedule: April 26–28, 2012, at the Hofstra Cultural Center in Hempstead, Long Island.

While in Port St. Lucie, relax and enjoy. The PGA has a cool museum and golf facility at the same I-95 exit as the spring-training complex, plus there are beaches to lie on and Savannas Preserve State Park to walk in. But many who travel to St. Lucie in March are there for one thing: Mets baseball. So slather on the sunscreen, buy the cheap seats on the outfield hill—they'll give you a hard time about sitting there if you don't have tickets for that section—or pay an extra $5 or so for better seats, get the Cubano sandwich at Bagel Brothers, and tipple back a cocktail at the Tiki Bar. If you're sticking around after the game, head to Duffy's, spend the night at neighboring SpringHill Suites or one of several other nearby hotels, and, if you're lucky, catch the monthly Mets Booster Club meeting, featuring special guests from the team. The ballpark souvenir shop is also a nice destination for those who simply must get that gift for someone back home who tells the world: "So and so went to spring training and all I got was this lousy tee shirt."

⚾ Mets Hall of Fame and Museum ⚾

One of the easier side trips a Mets fan can take is bypassing the escalator in Citi Field's Jackie Robinson Rotunda and strolling over to the Mets Hall of

Fame and Museum. Created in the wake of a fan backlash over the new ballpark's lack of Mets-centricity, the team responded with a thirty-seven hundred square-foot space to celebrate the club's lively romp through history.

Shea Stadium had a collection of busts for Mets who were inducted into the team's Hall of Fame—starting in 1981—but it was buried in a place where fans without Diamond Club passes rarely ventured. The busts have been replaced by plaques, and they went one better: after inducting no Met for eight years, in 2010 the Mets christened the museum by inducting four men crucial to the 1986 world championship—General Manager Frank Cashen, pitcher Dwight Gooden, Manager Davey Johnson, and outfielder Darryl Strawberry.

Interactive displays, trophies, memorabilia, and artwork from some of the most extensive Mets collections—as well as items donated by former players—make it well worth a few minutes before or after a game (and sometimes even during). This walk down memory lane is great for the longtime fan and those new to baseball to learn why the Mets resonate with so many people. The people asked for it, the people got it, and the people should enjoy this Amazin' museum.

The New York Mets Hall of Fame, Flushing, New York
Joan Payson, Owner 1960–1975; Inducted 1981.

Casey Stengel, Manager 1962–1965; Inducted 1981.

Gil Hodges, First Baseman 1962–1963; Manager 1968–1971; Inducted 1982.

George Weiss, President and General Manager 1961–1966; Inducted 1982.

William A. Shea, Mover and Shaker; Inducted 1983.

Johnny Murphy, Executive 1961–1967, General Manager 1968–1970; Inducted 1983.

Ralph Kiner, Broadcaster 1962–; Inducted 1984.

Bob Murphy, Broadcaster 1962–2003; Inducted 1984.

Lindsey Nelson, Broadcaster 1962–1978; Inducted 1984.

Bud Harrelson, Shortstop 1965–1977, Coach 1982, 1985–1990, Manager 1990–1991; Inducted 1986.

Rusty Staub, Outfielder 1972–1976, 1981–1985; Inducted 1986.

Tom Seaver, Pitcher 1967–1977, 1983; Inducted 1988.

Jerry Koosman, Pitcher 1967–1978; Inducted 1989.

Ed Kranepool, First Baseman/Outfielder 1962–1979, Inducted 1990.

Mets People

Jerry Seinfeld: "Jerry from Queens"

You couldn't have lived through the 1990s without seeing an episode or two—or all 180 episodes—of *Seinfeld*. The self-proclaimed "show about nothing" not only featured a raving-mad George Steinbrenner (the character always shown from behind), *Seinfeld* was also the brainchild of a dyed-in-the-wool Mets fan who shares a first name with Mets Hall of Fame "Jerrys" Grote and Koosman.

The Mets have been depicted throughout their history on television and in film. The Mets were Oscar Madison's team in the Broadway, film, and TV versions of *The Odd Couple*; Apu wore a Mets jersey on an episode of *The Simpsons* and proclaimed, "The Nye Mets are my favorite squadron"; "Meet the Mets" was sung on *Everybody Loves Raymond* (where the dog was named after 1969 Mets outfielder Art Shamsky); and, in *The King of Queens*, Doug Heffernan inadvertently ran on the field in an episode filmed at Shea Stadium and wound up in Mets jail, where he found his wife, who had spit on a beer vendor.

But the Mets were a recurring theme in *Seinfeld*, starting with the 1989 pilot episode. Jerry answered the phone, "If you know what happened in the Mets game don't tell me, I taped it. Hello?" It was the wrong number, but Kramer barged in and bellowed his first lines on the show, "Boy, the Mets blew it tonight, huh?" In the final half-hour episode of *Seinfeld*, nine years later, Mets announcer Bob Murphy served as background as Jerry and friends left a Mets game early, missed the club's big comeback, and got in plenty of trouble both on- and offscreen (Kramer's burning of the Puerto Rican flag caused the episode to rarely be seen in syndication).

The *Seinfeld* episode most associated with the Mets, however, starred Keith Hernandez. That 1992 appearance was ranked as the fourth-best episode in television history by *TV Guide*. Why? "I'm Keith Hernandez." The line was cooed by the former Mets first baseman after being coached by *Seinfeld* cocreator Larry David, a Yankees fan and the voice of Steinbrenner on the show.

> *"When a guy's head hits the desk, you know you are getting every last nickel out of that guy. He is working as hard as he can."*

Although out of the public eye by choice in his post-*Seinfeld* life, Jerry has been seen at Mets games more often than anywhere else. The longtime season-ticket holder is an occasional caller to Steve Somers at WFAN—"Jerry from Queens" fills some of the void in the radio cosmos left by the 2003 death of beloved WFAN caller "Doris from Rego Park"—and talks about everything from Mets management to Lady Gaga's lewd gesture that got her tossed from the first row and stashed in Jerry's vacant Citi Field suite in June 2010. Later that month, as a present from his wife, Jerry sat in for half a game in the SNY booth with Gary Cohen and, yes, Keith Hernandez. Jerry even got in the final word on Keith dozing off during an extra-inning game earlier in the season: "There's nothing wrong with falling asleep, by the way, on the job," he said as both announcers doubled over laughing. "Because when a guy's head hits the desk, you know you are getting every last nickel out of that guy. He is working as hard as he can."

Unlike the results in most of the Mets mentions on *Seinfeld*, the team won with Jerry in the booth. "Not that there's anything wrong with that."

Cleon Jones, Outfielder 1963–1975; Inducted 1991.
Jerry Grote, Catcher 1966–1977; Inducted 1992.
Tug McGraw, Pitcher 1965–1967, 1969–1974; Inducted 1993.
Mookie Wilson, Outfielder 1980–1989, Coach 1997–2002; Inducted 1996.
Keith Hernandez, First Baseman 1983–1989; Inducted 1997.
Gary Carter, Catcher 1985–1989; Inducted 2001.
Tommie Agee, Outfielder 1968–1972; Inducted 2002.
Frank Cashen, General Manager 1980–1991; Inducted 2010.
Dwight Gooden, Pitcher 1984–1994; Inducted 2010.
Davey Johnson, Manager 1984–1990; Inducted 2010.
Darryl Strawberry, Outfielder 1983–1990; Inducted 2010.

Appendix

The Places Called Home

HE METS HAVE CALLED three ballparks home in their fifty years as a franchise. Their first domicile was in Manhattan, while the other two have been on the same plot of land in Queens. More than one hundred million people have entered these homes to see the Mets in their half century of existence. Win or lose, the people keep on coming.

Polo Grounds (1962–1963)

The Polo Grounds was like moving into your parents' house after graduation. The place needed work after the Giants abandoned it to flee to the West Coast. The Mets spent $300,000 to refurbish the park, including a new scoreboard, paint, and replanted grass. The Mets officially reopened the joint on April 13, 1962.

Despite their hideous play, the Mets were new and fun, something young people could call their own and a break from the old tradition. Fans celebrated the game in new ways—with banners, signs, and slogans. The "New Breed" they were called—a name that also applied to the reporters who covered the club. The Mets held their own—attendance-wise, that is—even with the neighboring Yankees winning the pennant both years the Mets called Manhattan home. The Polo Grounds and Yankee Stadium were located a brief walk from each other, across the Macombs Dam Bridge that spanned the Harlem River, but the two teams were a universe apart in the standings. The Mets were 56–105 at home those two years—a brutal record, but not nearly as bad as the fledgling club's 35–126 mark its first two seasons on the road. Just when you thought nothing could ever be worse than the 1962 club's 120-loss debut, well, there you go.

The departed Giants and Dodgers were by far the biggest draws for the Mets at the Polo Grounds. Home games against those teams accounted for thirteen of the fourteen crowds exceeding thirty thousand in 1962 and 1963. In all, the Mets drew just under two million fans total during their two years at the Polo Grounds. That was middle of the pack for the National League at the time. A move to Queens did not improve the team's standing all that much, but a lot more fans came out, as the 1963 song went, to "Meet the Mets."

Shea Stadium (1964–2008)

If the newfangled Mets were a product of the New Frontier of the early 1960s, so was their ballpark. Built big, bright, and bold, it was also conveniently located adjacent to the World's Fair, which was held in Flushing Meadows in 1964 and 1965. New York's master builder Robert Moses, whose insistence that New York's next ballpark be built in Flushing eventually led to the exit of both the Dodgers and Giants, rewarded the Mets with the added bonus of a World's Fair next door. The spillover crowds helped the Mets draw 1.7 million in each of their first two years at the fifty-five-thousand-plus seat ballpark; only the Dodgers—the 1963 and 1965 world champions—drew more in that span. The Yankees, by contrast, drew almost a million fewer people than the Mets during 1964–1965. The Mets would outdraw the Yankees in each of their first twelve seasons in Flushing, including the two years both clubs shared Shea, 1974 and 1975.

By then, Shea had seen the two World Series, an All-Star Game, an AFL Championship Game, the Beatles, and numerous other headline events, but 1975 topped them all for sheer volume. Because Yankee Stadium was being rebuilt and Giants Stadium was still under construction, Shea served as 1975 home to the Mets, Jets, Giants, and Yankees, a total of 173 regular-season games—plus the annual Mayor's Trophy exhibition game between the Mets and Yankees. The city's financial crisis forced everyone to make do with what was available. The Yankees and Giants moved out in 1976, but the Jets stuck around Shea. The Jets had shared a stadium with the Mets dating back to the Polo Grounds—when New York's American Football League team was known as the Titans—but the Shea experience was not always a happy one for the Jets. Their second-banana status at Shea wore thin, and the Jets moved to New Jersey to share Giants Stadium after 1983.

New ownership spruced up Shea, removing the old wooden seats— and the iconic aluminum panels—while also installing DiamondVision, the Picnic Area, and the Home Run Apple. But it wasn't slogans on the outside of the stadium, Grucci fireworks, or even returning icon Tom Seaver that brought life back to Shea after seven down seasons. Winning transformed the place. K Korner, the wave, and curtain calls all arrived in New York when the Mets became a sudden contender in 1984, with wunderkind Dwight Gooden emerging as a teenage ace whose every start turned Shea into "the place to be." The first three-million-attendance season outside of Los Angeles was achieved the season after the Mets won the 1986 world championship. The Mets reached that attendance milestone again in 1988, though the team fell short of another World Series when the Dodgers beat them in the NLCS. Ironically, the Mets had beaten Los Angeles ten of eleven times during the 1988 season and had pushed past them for highest attendance in the game, the first time the Mets had held that distinction since the 1969 champions began a run of four straight seasons as the game's top draw.

Mets attendance decreased each year from 1989 through 1992, but baseball's popularity was such that attendance went up in 1993, a 103-loss season that saw the publication of a book on the team's horrific 1992 season, *The Worst Team Money Could Buy*. Baseball took a devastating blow with the 1994 strike. When play finally resumed in 1995, fans were slow coming back, especially to see the Mets. Though the 1997 Mets stayed in contention until the final week of the season, you still had to go back to 1976 to find a Mets team with a winning record that drew fewer than the 1997 club's 1.76 million fans. The Mets needed a marquee star . . . and they found one when they traded for Mike Piazza.

The Mets surpassed two million fans in each of Piazza's eight seasons in New York. But by the 2000s, with new stadiums throughout baseball making the game more enticing to the casual fan and those looking for creature comforts in their sports venues, three million fans were needed to land a team anywhere near the top of the heap in terms of attendance. And with the Mets owned by real estate developers—Fred Wilpon had bought out Nelson Doubleday in 2002—it was no secret that the team longed for a new stadium. Even as Shea broke its attendance mark three years running—the Mets drew 11.2 million from 2006 to 2008, including the club's only four-million-attendance season in 2008—the old ballpark's life was drawing to a close. On September 28, 2008, the Mets played their 3,570th and final game at Shea Stadium. Like their first game in Flushing, it was a loss, though the last game at Shea eliminated the Mets from contention. But for a franchise that was seventy-eight games under .500 after its first five seasons at Shea, a mark of 1,856–1,709–5 at home wasn't something to feel bad about. Sad? Maybe.

Citi Field (2009–Present)

Mets fans run both sentimental and practical. So when the new ballpark opened, the people spoke loudly about the things they did not like. Fans complained about the corners of the field being cut off from view in many seats, as well as the prices, the lines, the fans milling around all game long, the naming of the stadium after a bank that received government aid, and, most vociferously, the absence of a Mets motif from the new Mets park. The gripes had merit. After all, the team constantly reminded fans, this wasn't Shea. In Shea's inaugural season of 1964, a box seat in the state-of-the-art ballpark cost $3.50. Four and a half decades later, it cost upwards of one hundred times that amount for the best seats in the house. It didn't help that the oft-injured 2009 Mets stumbled through their worst season since 2003.

Mets fans are also a resilient bunch. Management worked to change the perception of the new stadium. The Ebbets-revival park became less Dodgers-centric, more images of Mets were hung, a Mets Hall of Fame and Museum was created in the Jackie Robinson Rotunda, the bridge in center field was renamed the "Shea Bridge," and the old Home Run Apple was moved outside the main entrance (a new Home Run Apple had been in place for Citi Field's opening, though the power-deprived offense had great difficulty in making it rise).

Built more like the spacious ballparks in San Francisco and San Diego than some of the cozier new eastern stadiums, Citi Field has required some getting used to for Mets fans—and a few players. Citi Field is home. It just may take some time for home to become sweet.

Shea Good-Bye Roll Call

For the final game at Shea Stadium, the Mets brought out former players who touched every era of the ballpark's forty-five seasons in the sun. The players were introduced one by one after the final game, and they lined up on either side of the diamond. Then they each touched home plate one last time. By the time Tom Seaver threw one last pitch to Mike Piazza, some people were so lost in the memories and the moment, it may have been hard to remember that they played just one game that day. And lost. Here's the dream roster of Mets of future past.

Jack Fisher	Howard Johnson
Ron Hunt	Bobby Ojeda
Al Jackson	Robin Ventura
Frank Thomas	Al Leiter
Jim McAndrew	Ed Kranepool
Ed Charles	Cleon Jones
Art Shamsky	Buddy Harrelson
Wayne Garrett	Jesse Orosco
George Theodore	Edgardo Alfonzo
Dave Kingman	John Franco
Felix Millan	Rusty Staub
Craig Swan	Lenny Dykstra
Doug Flynn	Gary Carter
John Stearns	Jerry Koosman
George Foster	Yogi Berra
Tim Teufel	Keith Hernandez
Todd Zeile	Darryl Strawberry
Ron Swoboda	Dwight Gooden
Lee Mazzilli	Willie Mays
Wally Backman	Mike Piazza
Ron Darling	Tom Seaver
Sid Fernandez	

The Annual Record

Mets Club	W	L	PCT	PLACE	MANAGER	ONE-LINE SUMMARY
1962	40	120	.250	10th	Stengel	*Can't Anybody Here Play This Game* wasn't just a book title, it was a legitimate question by Casey Stengel.
1963	51	111	.315	10th	Stengel	The Mets say farewell to the Polo Grounds, but losing would be harder to shake.
1964	53	109	.327	10th	Stengel	New stadium, World's Fair next door . . . what do you want, a sixty-win team, too?
1965	50	112	.309	10th	Stengel/Westrum	The first Mets team to backslide from the previous year—and backsliding from fifty-three wins is ugly.
1966	66	95	.410	9th	Westrum	The first non-triple-digit loss, non-last-place season . . . there is joy in Metville.
1967	61	101	.377	10th	Westrum/Parker	Two good things happened: Seaver arrived and Westrum left.
1968	73	89	.451	9th	Hodges	"Year of the Pitcher" meant even less offense at Shea, but the Mets were assembling a great staff.
1969	100	62	.617	1st	Hodges	From laughingstock to champion—there can never be another year like this.
1970	83	79	.512	3rd	Hodges	The Mets became just another club—no Miracles, just frustration.
1971	83	79	.512	3rd (Tie)	Hodges	One of Tom Seaver's most overlooked seasons, but it's remembered as the year Nolan Ryan was traded.
1972	83	73	.532	3rd	Berra	The third straight eighty-three-win season and the first year shortened by strike—a lost season and the season the Mets lost their leader, Gil Hodges.

Year	W	L	Pct	Finish	Manager	Notes
1973	82	79	.509	1st	Berra	Their win total goes down from 1972, yet they win a pennant and almost a World Series—"Ya Gotta Believe!"
1974	71	91	.438	5th	Berra	Waiting for the Miracle that never was and wouldn't come again for a long time.
1975	82	80	.506	3rd (Tie)	Berra/McMillan	Kingman clubbed thirty-six homers, Seaver won his third Cy Young, and still they barely reached .500.
1976	86	76	.531	3rd	Frazier	They never really competed, but it would be a while before they were this good again.
1977	64	98	.395	6th	Frazier/Torre	The Dark Age began on June 15 with the Seaver trade and wouldn't end until a full year *after* Seaver came back in 1983.
1978	66	96	.407	6th	Torre	Craig Swan won the ERA title and should've gotten a medal for leading this pitching staff.
1979	63	99	.389	6th	Torre	The third last-place year in a row, but they found a new owner with the start of the new decade.
1980	67	95	.414	5th	Torre	Magic? Not much, but sometimes there's magic just in having someone else run the store.
1981	41	62	.398	5th	Torre	Thanks to the strike, a split season gave the worse-than-mediocre Mets meaningful games in September.
1982	65	97	.401	6th	Bamberger	Bamberger replaces Torre . . . Joe's Braves win a division title while Bambi's Mets get slaughtered.
1983	68	94	.420	6th	Bamberger/Howard	Seaver was back, Hernandez arrived, and Orosco hit his stride, but contention was still a year away.

(*continued*)

Mets Club	W	L	PCT	PLACE	MANAGER	ONE-LINE SUMMARY
1984	90	72	.556	2nd	Johnson	"Day by day and almost minute by minute the past was brought up to date." —George Orwell, *1984*
1985	98	64	.605	2nd	Johnson	The second-best Mets team to date is second-best to the Cardinals.
1986	108	54	.667	1st	Johnson	"We haven't had that spirit here since 1969." —The Eagles, "Hotel California"
1987	92	70	.569	2nd	Johnson	Plenty of stick, arms call in sick.
1988	100	60	.625	1st	Johnson	Mike Scioscia, Orel Hershiser, and Bobby Ojeda's hedge clippers cut down the dream.
1989	87	75	.537	2nd	Johnson	When management 86ed the '86ers.
1990	91	71	.562	2nd	Johnson/Harrelson	End of the line for Johnson, Strawberry, and winning.
1991	77	84	.478	5th	Harrelson/Cubbage	"This is the bad time." —Ray Liotta, *Goodfellas*
1992	72	90	.444	5th	Torborg	Spend, spend, spend. Lose, lose, lose.
1993	59	103	.364	7th	Torborg/Green	The summer of 103 losses and countless humiliations.
1994	55	58	.487	3rd	Green	It was the worst of times for baseball but a nice improvement for the Mets.
1995	69	75	.479	2nd (Tie)	Green	They arrived late and fell on their face, but once out of contention, the 1995 Mets really started playing ball.
1996	71	91	.438	4th	Green/Valentine	Generation K goes down looking.
1997	88	74	.543	3rd	Valentine	Sometimes things change the most when you're really not expecting anything at all.
1998	88	74	.543	2nd	Valentine	Catch as catch can—dishing up Piazza behind the plate.

Year	W	L	Pct	Finish	Manager	
1999	97	66	.595	2nd*	Valentine	He who lives by October magic and walkoff wins can die the same way.
2000	94	68	.580	2nd*	Valentine	A real Subway Series: blood on the tracks.
2001	82	80	.596	3rd	Valentine	Where the defending NL champions—and everyone else—remember that baseball is just a game.
2002	75	86	.466	5th	Valentine	"Alomar Shrugged" or "Where There's Smoke, There's Fired."
2003	66	95	.410	5th	Howe	Howe could this happen?
2004	71	91	.438	4th	Howe	Oh, cruel contention of the imagination . . . at the cost of Kazmir.
2005	83	79	.512	3rd (Tie)	Randolph	*Pedro, Carlos, and Omar* was the title of a book and the "New Mets" were more fiction than fact.
2006	97	65	.599	1st	Randolph	A lead so big even the Mets couldn't blow it—until October.
2007	88	74	.543	2nd	Randolph	"I coulda had class, I coulda been a contender, I coulda been somebody, instead of a bum, which is what I am. Let's face it." —Marlon Brando, *On the Waterfront*
2008	89	73	.549	2nd	Randolph/Manuel	"This is the way the world ends/Not with a bang but a whimper."—T. S. Eliot, *The Wasteland*
2009	70	92	.432	4th	Manuel	The injury report was thicker than the yearbook.
2010	79	83	.488	4th	Manuel	Fans like Ike and are even warm to Jerry, but after the break, the season gets scary.
2011	77	85	.475	4th	Collins	Nothing was expected but Collins kept the team competitive—and Reyes tossed in a batting title.

*Won Wild Card

Index